CHINA AND THE UYGHURS

CHINA AND THE UYGHURS

A Concise Introduction

MORRIS ROSSABI

ROWMAN & LITTLEFIELD
Lanham • Boulder • New York • London

Published by Rowman & Littlefield
An imprint of The Rowman & Littlefield Publishing Group, Inc.
4501 Forbes Boulevard, Suite 200, Lanham, Maryland 20706
www.rowman.com

86-90 Paul Street, London EC2A 4NE

Copyright © 2022 by The Rowman & Littlefield Publishing Group, Inc.

All rights reserved. No part of this book may be reproduced in any form or by any electronic or mechanical means, including information storage and retrieval systems, without written permission from the publisher, except by a reviewer who may quote passages in a review.

British Library Cataloguing in Publication Information Available

Library of Congress Cataloging-in-Publication Data

Library of Congress Control Number: 2021944960

ISBN 9781538162989

CONTENTS

Preface		vii
Map of the Silk Roads		xiii
Acknowledgments		xv
1	Setting the Stage: Xinjiang and Imperial and Early Republican China	1
	Physical Environment	2
	Silk Roads	4
	Early History and the Silk Roads	5
	Mongol Era and Xinjiang to 1750s	9
	China Rules Xinjiang	14
	Rebellion in Xinjiang and Aftermath	16
	End of the Qing Dynasty and Consequences	22
2	China, the USSR, and the Emergence of Uyghurs	27
	USSR Involvement and Chinese and Uyghur Responses	30
	Chinese Communists Emerge Victorious	35
	New Communist Policies	37
	Repeated Changes in Communist Policies	49
	Emergence of Radical Initiatives	50

3 Moderation and Ensuing Violence, 1976–2000	*65*
Era of Reform in Xinjiang	*65*
Uyghur Protests Start in 1990	*74*
Government Responses to Protests	*77*
Increases in Violence and "Strike Hard"	*85*
4 "Carrots and Sticks" in the Twenty-First Century	*91*
Shanghai Cooperation Organization, 9/11 Aftereffects vs. Moderation	*91*
Uyghur Dissatisfaction and PRC Responses	*97*
Violent Explosions	*102*
Peace through Moderation or Strike Hard Policies?	*109*
Xi Jinping and Three New Policies	*115*
Xi Reacts to Violence	*120*
Training Centers or Camps?	*127*
Failures and Successes and the Future	*136*
US Policy	*139*
Bibliography	151
Index	157

PREFACE

Before the establishment of the People's Republic of China (PRC) in 1949 and its incorporation of regions in its northwest, the local inhabitants and China had a history of peaceful commercial relations, in part via the Silk Roads that linked it to the Middle East and Europe, and conflicts over governance in Eastern Turkistan and what the Chinese would call Xinjiang.[1] The region was frequently independent from 1911, the year of the fall of the Qing (or the last dynasty in China), and 1949, and the various Chinese governments, based in the capital cities of Beijing and Nanjing, did not truly control the area. After 1949, the PRC governed the area; and in 1955, it founded a Xinjiang Uyghur Autonomous Region (XUAR). The government encouraged and, at times, compelled Han (or ethnic Chinese) migration to the newly established XUAR, but starting in the 1990s Han settlers voluntarily moved into the XUAR's central areas because of greater economic opportunities.

Economic, ethnic, and religious problems between the PRC and the Uyghur Turks, Kazakhs, Hui (Chinese Muslims), Kyrgyz, Mongols, and other minorities in Xinjiang have, on occasion, led to violence. Some Uyghurs[2] and other non-Han in the region have requested greater autonomy in order to express their ethnic and religious identities and to avert oppressive PRC policies whereas others have little interest in politics. Still others who have done well in the XUAR have been satisfied with a more prosperous lifestyle and better access to modern education and medicine and would not mind assimilation. A few have demanded separation from China and total independence. The non-Han peoples are not monolithic in their attitudes toward the PRC and the Han. Yet enough of them bristle at Han rule and authoritarianism that the stage has been set for confrontation and violence. Many of the PRC leaders, believing that they have contributed to the economy, health, and education of the XUAR's inhabitants, have regarded the non-Han dissenters as unappreciative and as separatists and, in some cases, as terrorists.

China's plans, announced in 2013, for a Belt and Road Initiative, which would provide road, rail, and seaborne links to Europe, the Middle East, and Africa, have directed attention to the XUAR, which would, due to this development, regain, via the traditional Silk Roads, the stature it once held as an integral part of Eurasia. The XUAR has become particularly prominent because it is the main thoroughfare from China to Central and South Asia. Turfan, Urumchi, Kashgar, and other traditional oases and modern cities would serve as links to Eurasia for trade, development, and perhaps even cultural exchanges. The XUAR's Muslims, who constitute approximately half the population of Xinjiang, would be in closer contact with coreligionists in Central and South Asia and even as far away as Iran, Turkey, and the Arab world. The Han leaders have been concerned that instability in Xinjiang could undercut the Belt and Road regions.

They are aware of the complications that Xinjiang poses to the Belt and Road project. An unstable Xinjiang would subvert a critical section of this Eurasian link. Since the founding of the PRC in 1949, this so-called Autonomous Region has seen periods of considerable turbulence. On the one hand, the government, at various times, supported or turned a blind eye to the destruction of mosques, shrines, and cemeteries, demanded the study of the Chinese language for Uyghurs and other minority students in schools, imposed virtual martial law or resorted to violence in various towns, executed and allegedly tortured Uyghurs, censored the publication of Uyghur literature, and prohibited Muslim attire and diet. On the other hand, Uyghurs, whom the government labeled "splittists" and a few of whom were indeed extremists, killed policemen, soldiers, and ordinary citizens and placed bombs in public spaces in Xinjiang. They also initated attacks as far away from Xinjiang as the southwest Chinese province of Yunnan, the streets of Beijing, and a temple in Thailand.

Under these circumstances, it has been difficult to maintain a balance in describing the differing views, policies, and actions of the Uyghurs and the Han. The tumultuous events in Xinjiang have given rise, in particular, to the publication of numerous studies in the past few years. A few have dealt with nineteenth- and early twentieth-century Xinjiang, but an increasing number has focused on events since 1949. From 2017 on, many Western newspapers and magazines, including the *New York Times*, the *New Yorker*, the *Washington Post*, and the Communist-sponsored *Global Times*, have devoted an extraordinary amount of space to Xinjiang. Yet, in some of this reporting, staunch supporters of the Uyghurs, on occasion, have not emphasized or even mentioned the killings and bombings by Uyghur militants, while advocates for the PRC often ignore its repressive policies (imprisonment, executions) toward the Uyghurs. Loaded terminology such as "genocide," "atrocities," and "terrorists" frequently characterize these reports, and the sources are either not cited or not fully identified.

Two experts allude to another possible problem with sources: "Expatriates who seek a public voice generally advocate independence for Xinjiang and so they have powerful incentive to exaggerate the scope and intensity of Uyghur dissidence in an effort to muster support for their cause and pressure the PRC to change its policies. Furthermore, as expatriates, these sources cannot provide firsthand accounts of current events in Xinjiang."[3]

The Chinese government is partly to blame because it requires foreign journalists to secure permission to travel in Xinjiang and often has them followed or placed under surveillance. Journalists scarcely receive opportunities to interview local inhabitants and are often dependent on information that expatriates or anti-communists provide. The PRC government itself issues misleading and inaccurate reports and labels some Uyghurs who seek greater autonomy as terrorists.

This book will deal with Chinese policies toward the Uyghurs and other non-Han, especially during the era of President Xi Jinping, as well as the Uyghurs' reactions to these government initiatives. A balanced view is the ideal but difficult to achieve, and I do not claim that I have been totally successful in doing so. I will present the perceptions of the Han and the non-Han based on my own years of study of the region and of Inner Asia as a whole, as well as my previous publications, and I trust that my views will be of use to the general reader and perhaps to scholars in the field. I will humbly suggest some possible options for US actions, if any.

The book was written as a guide for general readers who seek information about Xinjiang, a seemingly remote part of the world. The conflicts between China and some of the local inhabitants in the region, Xinjiang's oil and mineral resources, and its location for the state's Belt and Road Initiative have contributed enormously to its significance. The work is based on my own research, as well as major studies by distinguished specialists, but it omits lengthy citations or numerous footnotes. Nonetheless, I provide a bibliography for readers who wish additional information about subjects addressed in the book. I provide a historical sketch of China's relations with Xinjiang, highlighting the most important developments. I omit less pertinent events and again refer the reader to the bibliography for additional details about specific periods in history.

Forty-five years ago, I concluded *China and Inner Asia*, my first book, which dealt with the Uyghurs, the Mongols, and the Manchus, with the following observation: "It is difficult to determine whether the [Chinese] Communists were wise in deciding to impose direct control over these areas. As one recent student of Communist policy toward the various minority nationalities concluded: 'Minority problems in most societies have proven enormously resistant to easy or rapid solutions, irrespective of the broad goals enunciated or the concrete policies applied. It is not yet clear that the People's Republic of China constitutes an exception."[4]

NOTES

1. The term "Xinjiang" came into wide use only in the nineteenth century, but for the sake of convenience and to prevent confusion for the reader, I will use it to describe earlier periods. Towns and cities in Xinjiang have been known by different names throughout history. I will most often use their present names. Turkic people have referred to it as Eastern Turkistan or Uyghuristan, and most continue to do so.

2. In the nineteenth and twentieth centuries, the Uyghurs have also been known as East Turkistanis, Altishahris, Kashgaris, and Taranchis. Only in the 1930s did the term "Uyghurs" gain wide currency. See chapter 2 for an explanation.

3. J. Todd Reed and Diane Raschke, *The ETIM: China's Islamic Militants and the Global Terrorist Threat* (Santa Barbara: Greenwood, 2010), 14.

4. June Dreyer, "Traditional Minority Elites and the CPR Elite Engaged in Minority Nationalities Work," in Robert Scalapino, ed., *Elites in the People's Republic of China* (Seattle: University of Washington Press, 1972), 450.

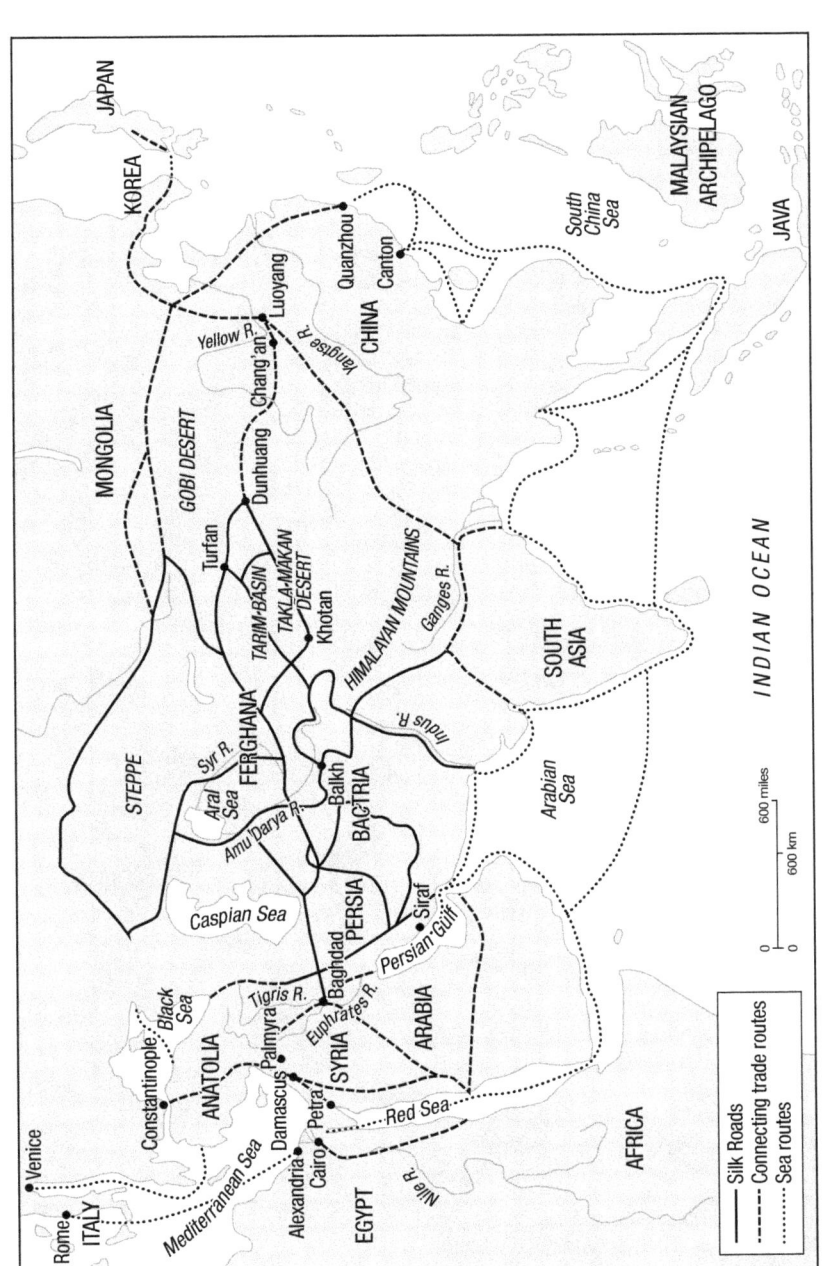

The Silk Roads

ACKNOWLEDGMENTS

I have incurred numerous obligations in the research and publication of this book. My greatest debts have been to the Uyghurs, Chinese, and Mongols who allowed me to interview them. They will remain nameless, but I cannot sufficiently thank them for their candor and often their hospitality. The Smith Richardson Foundation provided me with a fellowship that offered opportunity for travel and time to undertake the research and writing of this work, though the Foundation is not responsible for the views presented here. I am grateful to Professors Dru Gladney and Ildikó Bellér-Hann with whom I consulted about possible interviewees in this field. Professor Don Wyatt of Middlebury College and Professor Marsha Weidner of the University of Kansas invited me to give talks on my ongoing research. Professor Jeremy Murray of California State University at San Bernardino arranged for me to lecture at the University of Southern California, Pomona College, University of California at Los Angeles, University of California at San Diego, and California State University at San Bernardino mostly on the Mongols, but I also talked about my research on the Uyghurs. My wife and I traveled with Arienne Dwyer of the University of Kansas in Xinjiang, and she proved to be an invaluable guide to developments in the region, although she has differing views than I express here. These former and current students have been important sounding boards for the ideas presented in my books: Dr. Darren Byler of Simon Fraser University, Professor George Kallander of Syracuse University, and Professor Benno Weiner of Carnegie Mellon University. I am indebted to two anonymous reviewers who provided invaluable suggestions.

I have also been extraordinarily fortunate for fifty-five years of marriage to Mary, whose wit, intelligence, and public spirit has enriched both of our lives. The family we developed has been inspiring. I am grateful to Amy, Tony, Howard Sterinbach, Dr. Anna Rossabi, Sarah Sterinbach, Nathan Sterinbach, and Julia Rossabi for often humoring their father and grandfather.

CHINA AND
THE UYGHURS

1

SETTING THE STAGE

Xinjiang and Imperial and Early Republican China

Like the US and Russia, China has, throughout history, added to its domains. Also similar to Russia, it has, in enlarging the territory under its control, incorporated foreign groups with different languages, religions, customs, social structures, and economies. The greatest expansion was relatively late in Chinese history. Only in the Manchu Qing dynasty (1644–1911) did China consistently impose its power in areas along its present northern and western frontiers. The non-Han peoples along its borders did not voluntarily submit; the Qing conquered their territories. Inner Mongolia fell to the Manchus even before they started to rule as the Qing. By 1691, the Manchus compelled the submission of the Eastern Mongols, but the Zunghar or Western Mongols abandoned their lands and went to Tibet, which offered the Qing a pretext to launch an invasion. In 1719, Qing forces moved into Tibet and occupied and started to govern that Buddhist country for the only time in history, except for the Mongol invasions of the thirteenth and fourteenth centuries. Remnants of the Zunghar troops fled to the northwest region, which came to be known as Xinjiang. Yet again, after considerable preparations, in the 1750s Qing armies attacked and occupied the northwest region, which currently constitutes approximately one-sixth of China's total territory. By 1760, the Qing and, indeed, modern China had enormously expanded the lands under their control.

By incorporating non-Han peoples into China, the Qing and later Han governments have faced the minority issues that have also confronted Russia, the United States, and many other countries. Each has dealt with minorities in different ways, but many states have not resolved the majority-minority relationship. A brief history is required to understand the present Xinjiang-Han relationship.

PHYSICAL ENVIRONMENT

Xinjiang alone encompasses a territory of approximately the same size as Western Europe. Such a vast domain naturally consists of diverse landscapes, but Xinjiang includes more extremes than most other locations. Lofty mountains separate the region into distinct areas. The Tianshan, which covers much of the middle of Xinjiang, divides the south from the north and rises, in the west, to more than 23,000 feet. The Altai mountains in the northeast serve as the border with Mongolia, while the Kunlun, in the south, with one of its peaks at 28,000 feet, limits access to Tibet. Travelers in the southwest skirt the Pamir mountains, which reaches heights of more than 24,000 feet. Voyagers also face the Taklamakan, a daunting desert in the southern part of Xinjiang. This inhospitable desert compels travelers to journey either to its north or south and has led to the development of oases in both regions, which have eventually grown into towns.

The towns that lie on the fringes of the desert, such as Turfan and Hami in the north and Khotan and Yarkand in the south, are, for the most part, watered by the melting snows of the nearby mountains. In Turfan, one of the lowest points on Earth, with a harsh winter climate and excruciatingly hot and dry summers, the inhabitants devised an elaborate underground irrigation system known as *karez* to sustain themselves, their lands, and their animals. In the south, several smaller rivers wind up in the Tarim River, which flows north and west before heading into the dreaded Taklamakan. The capriciousness of the melting snows, on occasion, created crises and led to the abandonment of previously flourishing towns, another example of the fragility of this domain. In more modern times, and especially since the founding of the PRC, the government has developed water control and irrigation projects to foster agriculture and to protect the towns, but the motor-pumped wells have siphoned water from the *karez*. A growing population that has led to farming on less suitable land and the introduction of cotton have depleted the water supply, contributing to desertification. Extraction of oil and natural gas, which requires considerable water, has also impinged upon water resources, including those from the Tarim River.

Other than the extremes in landscape and climate, Xinjiang can be roughly divided into a north and a south. The north, or Zungharia (named for the Zunghar Mongols and also known as Yili), has traditionally been the home of the pastoral nomads and farmers. Like Mongolia, it has been blessed with abundant grasslands and has sustained roving groups who have a lifestyle based on animal husbandry. The North is also fortunate to have the Yili River, which permits a self-sustaining agriculture. The Yili flows westward and thus links Zungharia to Central Asia, especially to the country of Kazakhstan. Southern Xinjiang, which includes the Taklamakan desert and the Tarim River, boasts oases and towns, which have also maintained a self-sufficient agriculture. No insuperable obstacles come between north and south, which has enabled commercial relations between mostly pastoral peoples and town and oasis dwellers. Similarly, transport, via Xinjiang, to Central and South Asia and the Middle East is feasible, which makes the region a vital intermediary in trade and cultural and political relations throughout Eurasia. In modern times, Xinjiang borders on Mongolia, Russia, Kazakhstan, Tajikistan, Kyrgyzstan, Afghanistan, Pakistan, and India, contributing to its significance as a crossroads for trade.

SILK ROADS[1]

The Silk Roads were the main traditional thoroughfares for such Eurasian contacts. Caravans on the so-called Silk Roads conveyed luxury products; the more significant and vital commercial transactions were between nearby towns and pastoralists and hunters who exchanged necessities such as grain, horses, tea, and cloth. Nonetheless, some merchants and a few strategically situated oases and towns reaped considerable profits from long-distance Eurasian trade. Although the economic value of the Silk Roads trade may have been overestimated, its cultural significance was indisputable. It facilitated the spread of Buddhism and Islam and contributed to scientific, technological, and artistic diffusion throughout Eurasia. The routes differed depending on the way they averted the Taklamakan desert, and the route north of the desert eventually supplanted the rest. The main oases on this route were Hami, Turfan, and Korla and wound up in Kashgar before heading to Central Asia and Iran. The southern route, which linked China to India, wound its way through the towns of Khotan and Yarkand. A more modern route, which might more appropriately be labeled the "rhubarb road," developed in the seventeenth and eighteenth centuries. Believing that the wild rhubarb that grew in northwest China could resolve gastrointestinal disturbances, Europeans provided a substantial market for Russians whose territory was adjacent to the area and could transport the plant to Europe. The rhubarb route started at Kashgar, followed the Amu Dar'ya River north toward the Caspian Sea, then skirted that inland body of water, and headed to the Black Sea.

Long-distance trade required oases and towns, and a brief description of one such site reveals their significance. Hami, which the Chinese often called the gateway to the West, lay north of the Taklamakan. When such powerful Chinese dynasties as the Han (206 BCE–220 CE) and the Tang (617–907) controlled the town, the Silk Roads trade flourished. When China was not dominant, commerce declined. The population of the town was heterogeneous. Turks, Uyghurs,[2] and Mongols conquered the town, but the subjugated people remained. Different ethnic and linguistic groups, with such diverse religious beliefs as Buddhism, Nestorian Christianity, and Islam, coexisted, facilitating trade and cultural contact. The population had a subsistence agriculture. Like most of the other oases in the region, Hami was not highly fertile but relied on the waters descending from the Tianshan to sustain farming. The total population was relatively small; even as late as the Ming dynasty (1368–1644), it comprised several hundred households. Nor was it endowed with abundant natural resources. It owed its significance to its fortuitous geographical location, along the major trade routes. Its value for commerce and for defense motivated the more powerful Chinese dynasties to send troops to control the town, via garrisons and the establishment of postal stations. Few Han peoples actually settled in these oases and towns or in the northern pastoral areas after their service as guards. There is little evidence of a consistent Han presence in Xinjiang before the eighteenth and nineteenth centuries.

EARLY HISTORY AND THE SILK ROADS

In the past, Xinjiang has been known as Eastern Turkistan, a name often favored by Uyghurs seeking autonomy or an independent state. A variety of peoples passed through or inhabited the Tarim and Taklamakan areas. Indo-Europeans and Iranian speakers were among the first identifiable groups. So-called mummies, which were discovered in 2000 and have recently been publicized, attest to an Indo-European arrival in the area in prehistory and have led to controversies that have contemporary reverberations. Although the presence of Indo-European settlers had been known for decades, the publicity surrounding the discovery of the mummies aroused considerable consternation for the government. The PRC had sought to emphasize Xinjiang's long heritage as part of China. Discussion of the Caucasoid ancestry of the Urumchi mummies, as well as somewhat dissimilar mummies, appeared to challenge Han dominion over Xinjiang in earlier times. They indicated a non-Han presence in Xinjiang, a continued characteristic of the region's ethnic makeup throughout much of its history. The PRC has been concerned that the mummies could be used to question its claims to Xinjiang.

Additional PRC concerns derive first from the Han dynasty. A confederation known as the Xiongnu, who may have been related to the Huns, composed principally of nomadic pastoralist inhabitants, had arisen in Inner Mongolia, Mongolia, and modern northwest China around the third century BCE. Relations between the Han dynasty and the Xiongnu were often tense. They had different needs and strengths. The Xiongnu required grain and craft goods from China and thus supported trade, whereas the Han dynasty professed economic self-sufficiency. The Chinese had economic leverage. On the other hand, the Xiongnu cavalry offered advantages in hit-and-run raids and attacks on China to obtain goods the Xiongnu needed when the Han denied them commerce. Thus, they had military advantages.

The Han dynasty developed new policies designed to lead to peaceful relations with the Xiongnu, but none were entirely successful. One approach was a search for allies. Emperor Wu (r. 140–87 BCE), the most renowned Han emperor, dispatched an envoy named Zhang Qian to propose an alliance with a group whom the Xiongnu had defeated and had compelled to move to Western Central Asia. Having migrated a considerable distance from their original homeland, this group showed no interest in still another conflict with the Xiongnu.

Zhang's expedition was a dismal diplomatic failure, but it turned out to be an invaluable embassy. Zhang provided information about the regions he visited and offered his expertise to the court for several decades. His most significant report concerned the excellent horses he encountered in the so-called Western Regions (or Central Asia). Because the Chinese desperately needed horses for their defense and did not have sufficient pastureland to breed and rear animals, Zhang's account motivated them to obtain these superior steeds. At the same time, the silk and other products he provided as gifts inspired other groups in Central Asia to seek trade with China. Zhang's mission thus contributed to the so-called Silk Roads. The Han dynasty set up garrisons and *tuntian*, or military colonies, in Xinjiang to protect its frontiers, merchants, and caravans, but very few ethnic Chinese settled there, which undermines the PRC claim that during the Han dynasty China ruled Xinjiang. The dynasty's military domination of the region was sporadic, and the population was diverse and mostly non-Chinese.

The collapse of the Han dynasty in the late second and early third centuries CE and the resulting lack of unity did not halt contacts between China and Xinjiang. Trade, especially long-distance Silk Roads commerce, appears to have been reduced, but local commerce between Xinjiang oases and China persisted. These essential oases served as intermediaries in the transmission of Buddhism from South Asia to China. Indeed, cultural diffusion may have been the most significant contribution of the Silk Roads and the Xinjiang oases. The towns bordering the Taklamakan desert, especially Khotan and Dunhuang, were situated along the main trade routes, and, after their adoption of Buddhism, several followed the South Asian model and produced Buddhist paintings and sculptures in caves.

Unification of China under the Sui (581–617) and Tang (618–907) dynasties aroused greater Chinese interest and contacts with Xinjiang. The Tang imperial family was more receptive to the maintenance of relations with areas in western Central Asia and, indeed, with the rest of Asia. Arabs, Iranians, Southeast Asians, and Indians arrived by ship, and some reached the capital city of Changan (modern Xi'an). At the same time, the overland Silk Roads flourished, as foreigners from Central Asia and Iran offered so-called tribute to the Chinese emperors and court and then traded with Chinese merchants. China was exposed to a variety of products from Central Asia, Iran, and the Middle East, and Islam, Manicheism, Zoroastrianism, and Nestorian Christianity accompanied the merchants and attracted some Chinese adherents. Xinjiang was vital in these cultural and economic exchanges.

Land-based trade required secure and safe passage through Xinjiang, not an easy task. The Tang sporadically controlled Xinjiang oases and set up garrisons, but Turks, Tibetans, and Arabs repeatedly challenged Chinese domination. Despite such conflicts and political disruptions, Silk Roads commerce persisted. Merchants, mostly of Sogdian background who spoke an Iranian language, were willing to undertake the risks because of the profitability of such trade. In sum, the Tang, on occasion, occupied Xinjiang, but few Han actually settled there. Xinjiang remained the homeland of Turkic people, with an intermingling of Tibetan and Iranian speakers and a few Arabs. Of the numerous principal Turkic dynasties in Xinjiang, the Uyghurs were perhaps the most renowned. Not to be confused with the modern Uyghurs, the traditional Uyghurs resided in Mongolia and created an empire from about 744 to 840, with their own Khaghan or ruler. They adopted the Manichean religion, developed a written script, and built a capital city. The Kyrgyz, still another nomadic confederation, defeated and ousted the Uyghurs, compelling them to abandon Mongolia. Most fled to Xinjiang and established capitals in the towns of Beshbaliq and Qocho.

The collapse of the Tang in 907 and the rise of the Song (960–1279) dynasty, a deliberately lesser empire, coincided with a dramatic rise in the power of generally nomadic states, culminating in the ascendance of the Mongol Khanates. Yet the critical change in this era was the rise of Islam in the western regions of Xinjiang. Turkic groups adopted Islam starting in the tenth century, as the Qarakhanids, a possible branch of the Uyghurs, became Muslims. In the tenth and eleventh centuries, they compelled local inhabitants to convert to Islam or, in many cases, Xinjiang residents voluntarily adopted the religion. Yet Buddhism, the established religion in the region, did not initially disappear. As late as the fifteenth century, an envoy from the court of Tamerlane's son Shāhrukh noticed that a Buddhist temple was adjacent to a mosque in Hami, the gateway to the Silk Roads. Nonetheless, Islam generally eclipsed Buddhism as the major religion in Xinjiang.

MONGOL ERA AND XINJIANG TO 1750s

The ascendancy of Chinggis Khan (1162–1227) and the Mongols had a great impact on Xinjiang. Chinggis was afforded an opportunity to expand into Central Asia when a local governor massacred a Mongol caravan of four hundred of his merchants seeking to traverse this foreign terrain. The governor asserted that they were spies and had been dispatched to provide intelligence for a Mongol attack on his domain. Chinggis immediately demanded that the ruler of Central Asia turn over the governor for punishment. Instead, the ruler executed one of Chinggis's envoys. In 1219, the Mongol conqueror responded with a massive campaign, allegedly consisting of 200,000 troops, against Central Asia. Both sides were brutal. Some of the ruler's forces put up a stiff resistance, but by 1225, Chinggis's troops had emerged victorious, and Chinggis chose his son Chaghadai as the khan of Central Asia or Transoxiana.

Despite Chinggis's conquests in Transoxiana and the submission of the Uyghurs in southern Xinjiang, tensions persisted in both regions through the era of Khubilai Khan (r. 1260–1294) and beyond. Divisions among the Mongols undermined efforts to rule these areas, which included western Central Asia; Xinjiang, which the Uyghurs inhabited; and Zungharia, in modern northern Xinjiang, the home of pastoral nomadic peoples. Such hostilities contributed to disarray in Xinjiang and to Khubilai's inability to rule in the area, except for the allegiance of the Uyghurs.

The Mongols gained from their contacts with the Uyghurs. They adopted the Uyghur script for their written language and recruited Uyghur administrators, scribes, and financial experts. The Uyghurs' administrative skills, which were honed during their empire in the eighth and ninth centuries, served them and the Mongols well. Gaining the trust of the Mongols, they enjoyed considerable self-rule. In any event, distance from the Mongols' Yuan dynasty capital in Daidu (or Beijing) and the desert and other demanding terrain that separated China from Xinjiang limited the possibility of direct and close governance over the region. The Uyghurs' towns in Xinjiang flourished with the Mongols' encouragement of trade until wars between Khubilai Khan and his cousin Khaidu erupted. Battles between the two flared up in Xinjiang, as well as in the Mongols' homeland in Mongolia, preventing China from dominating in Xinjiang.

The end of the Mongol era in 1368 offers an opportunity to review the relations between China and Xinjiang. Until the fourteenth-century demise of Mongol rule, few Han inhabited Xinjiang, whose population consisted mostly of Iranians, Turks, and Mongols. The Han who reached the region were mostly soldiers in some of the towns or oases or guards in encampments designed to protect voyagers traveling along the Silk Roads. China certainly did not rule Xinjiang. The inhabitants were frequently independent and had their own governments. If they were beholden to China, as in the Mongol era, they had considerable self-rule. It is difficult to accept the contentions of PRC historians and officials that China ruled Xinjiang from the Han dynasty on. A more accurate depiction is that the more powerful Chinese dynasties gained sporadic influence over Xinjiang, but they were unable to persuade many Han to relocate in the region. Xinjiang remained the homeland and under the control of non-Han peoples. Trade and so-called tribute linked China and Xinjiang during the height of the Silk Roads era, but a claim that Xinjiang was part of China would be misleading.

In the post-Mongol periods, until China's conquest in the 1750s, Xinjiang was generally not unified. One factor in such disunity was the lack of a regular and orderly system of succession to leadership, which often precipitated conflicts and weakened the various areas in Xinjiang. Another factor was the relatively unstable political environment, leading to a decline in long-distance trade, which had benefited the local inhabitants. Short-distance commerce persisted, but long-distance trade did not. The cultural, religious, and artistic diffusion that had characterized the Mongol empire was, as a result, curtailed.

In Central Asia, Tamerlane (or Temür) organized an army in the 1360s and conquered most of the region. He retained the Chaghadai Khan, a Mongol, as a ceremonial figure, but real power was in his hands, although he never adopted the title of "khan." He then annexed Iran and parts of the Middle East and Russia and recruited mostly Iranians to establish an administration to assist in ruling the vast domain he had subjugated. Toward the end of his life, he heard rumors that the Ming (1368–1644), the indigenous Chinese dynasty that had succeeded the Mongols, were persecuting Muslims. A fervent believer in Islam, Tamerlane prepared for an invasion to the east. En route to China, however, he died in 1405, and a struggle for succession precluded a second invasion of the Ming. Shāhrukh, one of Tamerlane's sons, emerged victorious and sought a more peaceful relationship with China.

In the east, Moghulistan's rulers in Xinjiang were also not unified, and dynastic struggles plagued them. One potentially unifying force was the Islamization of the region by the sixteenth century. Earlier, these areas had developed commercial relations with Ming China. The Chinese sources depict them as offering tribute to the Ming dynasty court and as vassals of China. Again, this is misleading. These areas were independent but sought trade and were willing to acquiesce to Chinese rituals in order to obtain essential and luxury products. The towns of Hami and Turfan were Xinjiang's main trading partners with the Ming. In the early sixteenth century, Turfan's rulers gained control over many nearby towns and oases. Ming China clearly did not govern Xinjang.

The seventeenth century witnessed an internationalization of issues relating to Xinjiang. Tsarist Russia appeared in Northeast Asia, as Russians colonized Siberia, reaching the Pacific Ocean at the port city of Vladivostok in 1648. At the same time, a Zunghar or West Mongol ruler named Galdan challenged the Qing dynasty in China, which had deposed the Ming dynasty and which had been established by the Manchus in 1644. The Zunghars raided near the northwestern border of China and occupied territory in

Xinjiang, particularly the pasturelands in the north, and Galdan sought to unify the Mongols. Trade and territorial disputes arose between the Qing and Galdan, leading to raids and battles.

Galdan had hoped to gain Russian support, but the Russians were much more interested in a harmonious relationship with China, which would mean access to such Chinese goods as tea, silk, and rhubarb. Tensions among the three parties enmeshed Northern Asia until Russia and China signed the Treaty of Nerchinsk in 1689, which delineated the Russo-Chinese border and permitted Russian trade with China. Galdan, who had contemplated cooperation with Russia, was now increasingly isolated, and Qing forces pursued and finally defeated him in 1696. His nephew led the surviving Zunghars to Tibet, where they dominated secular affairs while allowing the Dalai Lama religious authority. Still perceiving the Zunghars as a threat, the Qing decided on a campaign to oust them from Tibet. After considerable preparations to set up supply lines and to determine the logistics, Qing forces reached Tibet and defeated the Zunghars and established control in 1720.

Other Zunghars had fled to Xinjiang in the early eighteenth century after the fall of Galdan and sporadically controlled Hami, Turfan, and other towns. Nearly all of Xinjiang's population had adopted Islam, prompted by the activities of Sufi masters who allegedly had abilities to perform magic, to cure the sick, and to protect believers. Makeshift shrines, as well as elaborate tombs of saintly leaders, became centers for worship. Often led by religious leaders, the inhabitants of Xinjiang had considerable self-rule. Peace reigned until 1752, when succession struggles, a perennial problem for nomadic pastoralists and oasis dwellers from earliest times, plagued them. The Qing dynasty saw an opportunity to capitalize on these conflicts, and after considerable logistical efforts, unleashed a devastating assault that ended with China's first significant occupation of Xinjiang. The Zunghars disappeared as an identifiable group. A few Zunghars succumbed to a smallpox epidemic; some fled and joined Mongol groups to the west; some probably remained in Xinjiang and intermarried with other inhabitants and adopted their spouses' identities.

CHINA RULES XINJIANG

The mid-eighteenth-century Qing invasion and occupation marked the first time that a dynasty from China ruled all of Xinjiang. Yet nearly the entire population of Xinjiang was non-Han, and few Han would settle in the area. The current PRC claims that the Han ruled Xinjiang from the first century BCE is historically inaccurate; only in the 1750s did China truly rule Xinjiang. The Qing court dominated military in the region, but it allowed Xinjiang considerable self-rule.[3] The court appointed local Muslim officials known as *begs*, who frequently collaborated with the Qing, to administer local regions. The *begs* often governed large tracts of land and had the laborers to farm the land. Moreover, the Qing needed assistance in maintaining peace and in covering some of the costs for the military stationed in Xinjiang, and it turned to the *begs* and its own military forces to maintain control and to reduce expenditures.

The Qing court's objectives and its instructions to its officials were designed to avoid overly oppressive rule over the native inhabitants, yet difficulties would arise. The court sought to prevent too many Han from migrating to Xinjiang and did not wish to countenance repression of or discrimination against Islam, the faith of the vast majority of the population. Yet it could not lure capable officials from the central core of China to serve in such a remote region as Xinjiang. It was, on occasion, forced to rely on officials who had been accused of mismanagement, corruption, or other offenses, who were not eager to be situated in Xinjiang, and who were clearly unsympathetic toward Islam. Some capitalized on their positions to enrich themselves through corruption and graft. Even so, relative calm and economic development persisted for almost a century.

Conflicts arose from Central Asia. Religious leaders known as khojas who were associated with the Sufi orders of Islam resented rule by non-Muslims and believed that the Qing oppressed the local inhabitants in Xinjiang. Rebellions, which involved religious issues as well as trade and territorial disputes, erupted as early as 1781. The Qing sought to end the conflicts by negotiating an agreement with Khoqand, the nearest Central Asian state. It signed a treaty with Khoqand in 1832, which provided economic advantages for the Central Asians.

Xinjiang's local population did not, at first, challenge Qing rule. Commerce that Han merchants initiated contributed to a better economy for the Muslim elites, as did advances in agriculture due, in part, to new technology from China. Evidence is considerable that the *begs*, or local elite leaders, profited from trade with China. Most of the local population, however, barely eked out a living. The elite collected the region's products and provided jade, horses, livestock, cotton, and grain in return for silver and other valuables from the rest of China, and part of the silver was used for support of the Qing forces. Only as the Qing dynasty declined and trade possibilities diminished did the *begs* and other leaders begin to rupture their alliance with China. From 1760 to 1860, the native population scarcely initiated violence and generally accepted governance from China, which allowed it considerable self-rule. Khojas, as Muslim religious figures, led attacks, some with Central Asian assistance, in the 1840s and 1850s, but they were eventually suppressed. The PRC has pointed to the relative quiescence of the local Turkic peoples during this time to support its claim that the lack of challenge to rule from China indicated acceptance of such governance.[4]

REBELLION IN XINJIANG AND AFTERMATH

The rebellion that erupted in 1862 in northwestern Chinese provinces adjacent to Xinjiang and then spread to Xinjiang itself was not initially linked to the indigenous Turkic peoples. Chinese Muslims or Hui, who were also known as Dungans, were the original rebels who acted in opposition to official corruption and the overtaxation of both Han and Turkic peoples in the Chinese northwestern provinces. Then, Ya'qub Beg, a Khoqandian military leader from Central Asia, capitalized on the tumult to conquer and occupy towns and oases and become the ruler of southern Xinjiang by 1865. He imposed a harsh and authoritarian rule, doling out severe punishments on dissenters and strictly enforcing traditional Muslim practices and laws. He did not gain control over northern Xinjiang. Instead, Tsarist Russia, which had gradually expanded into Central Asia throughout the nineteenth century, moved troops into Yili in 1871, in northern Xinjiang, and stated that it would relinquish the territory once the Qing achieved stability in the area.

The Qing now faced two potential adversaries in Xinjiang and needed to make decisions concerning its policies toward an expansive territory, which it had incorporated into China a hundred years earlier. Ya'qub Beg naturally posed the greatest threat because he had detached 10 percent or more of the Qing's lands. Yet Xinjiang was far away from the capital in Beijing and from the center of Chinese civilization, and the court also confronted the apparently more pressing concerns of the Western nations, which had been making greater economic and diplomatic demands once

Britain's victory in the Opium War of 1839 to 1842 had revealed China's weakness. Most Qing officials acknowledged that China could not undertake two separate campaigns against its enemies, the Turkic peoples in Xinjiang and the Western countries along the east coast. The Qing would have to choose one campaign, and it would seem that defense of the traditional homeland, the east coast and the other central areas, would have been the optimal decision. Li Hongzhang, who acted as the equivalent of the foreign minister, advocated just such a policy.

The military leader Zuo Zongtang presented a counterargument. He recognized that Xinjiang was not a key economic center, but he asserted that China had always been attacked and conquered from the north and never from the south, where the ships from the Western countries landed. He stated that if China abandoned Xinjiang, a domino effect would follow. One northern province after another would fall to the Muslims in Xinjiang. On the other hand, Britain, France, and the other Western powers did not intend to annex territory and instead sought better conditions for trade. Thus, the real threat was in Xinjiang. This debate between Zuo and Li, two prominent statesmen, persisted for some years, but in 1874, the Qing, which had devoted substantial resources in the seventeenth and eighteenth centuries to annex territory along its western frontiers, supported Zuo to avoid relinquishing the region it had so arduously fought to incorporate. The court apparently considered Xinjiang an integral part of China and ordered Zuo to oust Ya'qub Beg.

After extensive preparations, Zuo's troops set forth in 1876. Ya'qub Beg temporized and tried to work out a compromise with the Qing, but Zuo's forces moved forward and almost inexorably captured one town after another. In 1877, Ya'qub Beg suddenly died. Resistance to the Qing melted away, and by early 1878, Zuo's troops had gained control over southern Xinjiang.

The next step after this resounding victory was recovery of Yili or northern Xinjiang. The Russian court, which had sent troops there allegedly to prevent the chaos, killing, and destruction in southern Xinjiang from spreading, had acted as if Yili would be no different from its other nineteenth-century territorial gains, such as modern Uzbekistan and Kazakhstan in Central Asia. It had encouraged Russians to settle in the area and even constructed a Russian Orthodox Church. Yili might, in time, become part of the Tsarist empire. The Qing could not tolerate such a loss. The Russians were actually in a weak position because they had had a debilitating war with the Ottoman empire. Moreover, Britain, which was engaged in the so-called Great Game, a struggle with Russia concerning their spheres of influence in Central and South Asia, and France pressured the Tsarist court to abide by its assurance in 1871 that it would return Yili to Qing control as soon as peace prevailed.

Zeng Jize, the son of a renowned official who had helped to crush the Taiping rebellion against the Qing, took charge of the negotiations and secured a good result in the Treaty of St. Petersburg of 1881. Under the terms of this new agreement, China first paid a sum that the Tsarist court sorely needed to replenish its coffers after the war with the Ottoman empire. It also made concessions, allowing the Russians to establish two consulates in Xinjiang and agreeing to a border demarcation that favored the Tsarist court. Yet the Russians withdrew from Yili, a victory for the Qing, though they would continue to play a role in the affairs of Xinjiang, their neighbor, from this time forward. Part of this involvement stemmed from the migration of Turks from Kashgar to Khoqand and other Central Asian areas in Russia after Zuo Zongtang's occupation of Xinjiang. After the Treaty of 1881, many other Turkic groups, including the Taranchis who had been peasants in Yili, moved to Russia. The Sino-Russian frontier was exceptionally fluid, as Turkic Muslims from Xinjiang crossed the border and interacted with other Turkic Muslims in Russia.

Despite the Qing's victory, the status of Xinjiang was still problematic. Although it was a part of the Qing empire, should it continue to be ruled as a virtual colony of China? Such a policy had not generated peace, especially when economic conditions worsened or when the court decided to levy additional taxes on Xinjiang. The creation of a regular bureaucracy could potentially lead to stability. If the court adopted that path, the optimal decision would be to designate Xinjiang as a regular province and not a colony. This status would translate into a reduction in military outlays and into opportunities for a closer connection between Xinjiang and other regions in China. Han migration into Xinjiang was integral to this policy, which might translate into greater assimilation of the local population with Chinese culture.

In 1884, the court officially designated Xinjiang as part of the provincial system, the beginnings of a new policy. Qing officials began to replace the local leaders in the government, thus impeding self-rule, and the court provided incentives for Han to move and settle in Xinjiang, but few Han actually migrated. The court strenuously sought to promote assimilation of the local peoples through acculturation and Sinicization. These heavy-handed approaches did not succeed. Most local inhabitants did not learn the Chinese language or show interest in Chinese culture. The Turkic population's rejection of the Qing dynasty initiatives was based on the perception that they aimed at gradual erosion of the local inhabitants' languages, culture, and religion, a common refrain that persists to the present.

Such threats were of particular concern because Islam underlay much of their culture and society. Sinicization, with its concomitant link to Confucianism, posed a challenge to Islam, which the local inhabitants resented. Muslims would be hostile to attempts to undercut or prohibit dietary practices, clothing, and patterns of worship. Islam was pervasive in the inhabitants' pilgrimages to *mazars*, or Sufi shrines, to pray for a better life or health or for children; their attendance at mosques; their educations at madrassas or theological schools; their festivals; their clubs or discussion groups called *mäshräp*; and their calls to prayer. The shrines, which housed texts about the lives of Sufi saints, contributed to the identities of the Muslim Turkic peoples. Leaders known as *shaykhs* cared for the shrines, prayed, and told stories about the Sufi heroes. Pilgrims would provide donations for the upkeep of the shrines and for the livelihood of the *shaykhs*.

The Qing court's decline after the Opium War of 1839–1842 with Britain exacerbated its difficulties in Xinjiang. Wars with Britain and France from 1858 to 1860 and with France in the 1880s and the Sino-Japanese War of 1894–1895, as well as rebellions, including the Panthay in the province of Yunnan from 1847 to 1878, the Taiping from 1850 to 1864, the Nian from 1853 to 1868, the Northwest Muslims from 1862 to 1878, and finally the Boxer of 1900, weakened the Qing, diverting attention and resources from Xinjiang. At the same time, corruption and bribery undermined Qing officialdom and, similarly, characterized the authorities in Xinjiang. Under these circumstances, the Qing would have faced difficulties with whichever policy it adopted. It could not devote itself to a region so far from the central territories, which required the greatest attention due to foreign threats and domestic turbulence.

This failure would set the stage for Xinjiang's relative independence in the early twentieth century. Xinjiang did not serve as a magnet for Han settlers. Instead, local inhabitants were the farmers who produced cotton and grapes and other fruits, among other crops, and the herders who provided animals and animal products. The one part of the economy in which the Han played a role was commerce. Han merchants brokered trade between Xinjiang and adjacent Chinese provinces. Another important development was Russian involvement in trade. Capitalizing on the favorable provisions in the Treaty of St. Petersburg of 1881, including the establishment of consulates, Russian merchants initiated trade within Xinjiang, yet again the beginning of a trend that would be controversial and troublesome for China, even into the Communist period.

In addition to Russia, Ottoman Turkey would have some influence in Xinjiang. Reformers in Turkey had focused their desire for change on Jadidism, to be described later, as the road to modernization. Jadidism spread to Central Asia and even to Xinjiang. Some reforms were introduced in a few regions in Xinjiang, not throughout the area, but no major Pan-Turkic movement developed, as it would in the pre–World War I Middle East.

Swedes constituted another major foreign group in Xinjiang in the late nineteenth century. Some were adventurers eager for excitement by journeying in the daunting terrain of the Silk Roads, while others were archaeologists, art historians, or historians fascinated by the arts, languages, and religions characteristic of the vast Eurasian domain. The Swedish Mission Society, which was founded in 1892, with branches in Kashgar, Yengissar, and Yarkand, sought to convert the local inhabitants to Christianity.[5] It failed in its original intent but played a valuable role in fostering education, publication, and research on Turkic languages and folklore. For example, Gustaf Raquette, a medical missionary at the Swedish Mission Society, was so fascinated with the area that he wrote important works on the native languages and cultures. The expeditions of Sven Hedin from 1893 to 1935 along the Silk Roads and in Tibet, Iran, and Mongolia brought considerable attention to Xinjiang.[6] His death-defying undertakings were, on occasion, irresponsible and, indeed, led to fatalities, yet they contributed to knowledge of the region. He trekked through the forbidding Taklamakan desert to find lost cities, remarkable Buddhist sites, and ancient military garrisons. He mapped much of this inaccessible area and gathered up coins, tools, and writings on wooden slips and dispatched them to Sweden.

Other foreigners followed in the path of Sven Hedin. They were fascinated by the ancient history of Xinjiang and northwest China but were also eager to transport its most beautiful artistic works to their own lands and museums. The explorer and adventurer Aurel Stein stumbled across the great Buddhist caves at Dunhuang in northwest China and gathered up texts and artifacts that he eventually gave to the British Museum, paving the way for the French scholar Paul Pelliot, who collected works from Dunhuang that wound up in the Musée Guimet in Paris. The German Albert von le Coq reached the caves in the Flaming Cliffs near Turfan and carved out sculptures that he sent to the Ethnological Museum in Berlin. The Japanese Buddhist Kōzui Ōtani gathered Buddhist artifacts at the Kizil Caves about forty miles northwest of Kucha and at Khotan, and the Russian Pyotr Kuzmich Kozlov collected objects and texts from the ruins of the Tangut people's capital of Khara Khoto in northwest China and dispatched them to St. Petersburg. These expeditions brought considerable attention to Xinjiang and popularized and romanticized the so-called Silk Roads. Nonetheless, their leaders carted away, with impunity, some of the great cultural treasures found in Xinjiang.

END OF THE QING DYNASTY AND CONSEQUENCES

The collapse of the Qing dynasty in 1911–1912 exacerbated the difficulties that had plagued Xinjiang in the late nineteenth century. Tensions and conflicts alternated with unity in relations between the Turkic peoples in southern Xinjiang, or Kashgaria, and the groups in northern Xinjiang and Central Asia known as Taranchis. After battles among military men and secret societies, a Han official named Yang Zengxin emerged victorious in Xinjiang. Yuan Shikai, the military man who became president of China in 1912, sought to retain Han control of Xinjiang but was barely able to rule over the central part of China, not to mention such a distant location as Xinjiang. Nonetheless, he "appointed" Yang as governor of the area, though Yang was an independent warlord.

After defeating his rivals in a brutal manner, Yang imposed a harsh authoritarian regime. Spies and censorship helped him retain control, and he murdered and executed recalcitrant dissenters or enemies. He promoted some economic developments, but most of the wealth accrued to him and to the Turkic leaders of the local inhabitants who had general jurisdiction over their own people, most of whom remained poverty-stricken. Yang sought to employ the local non-Han elites to keep the peace in their communities and was determined to maintain good relations with the Muslim leaders who provided him with the revenue for government, as he did not receive funding from the central governments. During his tenure, there was no sustained unrest by the local inhabitants, most of whom were Muslims. Yang rewarded them by repeatedly decrying Han chauvinism against minorities. The local communities, therefore, appear to have accepted rule by a Han, who resembled the warlords ruling a number of provinces in China. Nor did Yang face threats from other warlords or the Chinese government until Chiang Kai-shek's consolidation of power over much of the country in 1927–1928.

Before 1928, the year of Yang's death, the principal cause of unrest entailed relations with Russia and the USSR. After the 1881 Treaty of St. Petersburg, the Russians had established consulates in several cities in Xinjiang, and their merchants had developed a lively trade in the region. World War I and the Bolshevik

Revolution of 1917 not only subverted their commercial bonds, but also created a quandary, as Muslim Taranchis in Central Asia refused, in 1916, to be drafted into the Tsarist army to fight in Europe, and instead many moved into Xinjiang. In the next few years, White Russians who opposed the Bolsheviks fled from the onrushing Red Army and sought sanctuary in Xinjiang. Fearful of involvement in a civil war, Yang forced thousands of them to return to their homeland, where the communist Red Army would punish and, in some cases, execute them. Some slipped away and settled in different regions in Xinjiang, where they would remain until the Chinese Communist revolution.

Yang adopted a policy of peaceful relations with the Soviet Union and provided grain and other supplies to assist in warding off a famine in Central Asia and Russia in the early 1920s. By the mid-1920s, commerce with the USSR had been restored, and the two sides established consulates in each other's lands. Railroads and roads were constructed that linked Central Asia to Xinjiang. In fact, Xinjiang was closer geographically and economically to the USSR than to Chiang Kai-shek's central government, with its capital in Nanjing in eastern China. In addition, most of the people across the Xinjiang frontiers in the Central Asian regions of the USSR spoke Turkic languages akin to the Turkic spoken in Xinjiang; and the vast majority, like the people in Xinjiang, were Muslims. Yang was, however, concerned that interaction between Turkic peoples in Central Asia and Xinjiang would lead to the radicalization of his own people. He worried that trade between the two areas would allow the USSR undue influence in Xinjiang and perhaps permit Russians to lay claim to parts of the region.

Yet he had more immediate and pressing concerns that eventually led to his downfall. His authoritarian governance had rankled many in his own hierarchy. His brutal rule, together with increasing eruptions of local political activism, elicited enemies. The culmination of such dissatisfaction was his assassination in 1928, engineered in part by a warlord named Feng Yuxiang known as the "Christian General," who controlled much of north central China. The leader of the assassination plot did not emerge victorious. Instead, Jin Shuren, one of Yang's men, defeated the coup leaders and executed the main protagonist. Unlike Yang, his mentor, Jin, undermined Han relations with the local inhabitants. He attempted to curb the powers of the local Turkic leaders who had supported Yang and instead sought to build up his own military force to defend against warlords outside of the province. Yang had not interfered with the internal governance and beliefs of the non-Han. Jin abandoned this policy and prevented Muslims from practicing some of the obligations of their religion. At the same time, he encouraged Han to migrate to Xinjiang, which further alienated the non-Han groups.

Violence erupted, as rebellions broke out in several oases and towns. Part of this disorder stemmed from Jin's pressure on the non-Han, but the growth of indigenous Uyghur nationalism, which became a force at this time, also contributed to renunciation of Jin's leadership. Uyghur identity, which had been brewing among the Uyghur émigrés in the USSR, began to spread to Xinjiang. The outbreaks in the oases and towns, which the indigenous population led, weakened Jin, and the ensuing involvement of Hui, or Chinese Muslims, from China's northwestern provinces added to the tumultuous conditions. Jin was unable to control the new forces that sprang from a more resounding ethnic identity among Xinjiang's non-Han population, the origins of which will be considered in chapter 2.

NOTES

1. Much of this section derives from "Trade Routes in Inner Asia," which I completed in 1975, based on a commission from Professor Denis Sinor for the *Cambridge History of Inner Asia*, volume 2, which was never published.
2. These Uyghurs were not the same people as the modern Uyghurs.
3. James Millward, *Eurasian Crossroads: A History of Xinjiang* (New York: Columbia University Press, 2007), 101.
4. Although the rulers were Manchus, not Han peoples.
5. See Ondřej Klimeš, *Struggle by the Pen: The Uyghur Discourse of National and National Interest, 1900–1949* (Leiden: Brill, 2005), 82, for a brief notice of its activities.
6. His reputation suffered as a result of his pro-German views and his alleged support of Nazi Germany. For this, see Sarah Danielson, *The Explorer's Roundup to National Socialism: Sven Hedin, Geography, and the Path to Genocide* (Farnham, UK: Ashgate, 2012), 5.

2

CHINA, THE USSR, AND THE EMERGENCE OF UYGHURS

Starting in the 1920s and perhaps as early as the late nineteenth century, most of the non-Han Turkic peoples in Xinjiang began to coalesce around a so-called Uyghur identity, which referred to the Uyghurs, a Turkic group that ruled Mongolia from 744 to 840. After the Uyghur government's collapse, many of its people moved to Xinjiang and played a critical role there. However, the term "Uyghur" was no longer used after the middle of the Ming dynasty, in the sixteenth century, as groups not directly descended from the Uyghurs arrived in Xinjiang and intermarried with them. A connection with the old Uyghur state eroded and scarcely existed by the early twentieth century. Turkic nationalism, in the forms of the Young Turk movement in Turkey in the pre–World War I period and the modernization movement in post–World War I Turkey, aroused Turkic speakers elsewhere and had some impact in Xinjiang.

Perhaps more critical in the development of a Uyghur identity was the influence of the Tsarist and Communist policies toward nationalities in Russia and the USSR. In the late nineteenth and early twentieth centuries, groups from Xinjiang, seeking to avoid the turbulence in the region, had moved to Russia, which was starting to identify the various Turkic and Iranian groups within its expanding domains. This migration from Xinjiang started to generate a distinct Uyghur identity that was distinguished from other Turkic peoples. "Uyghur" intellectuals and merchants, numbering as many as one hundred thousand, had settled in Russia, where they were exposed to nationalist currents from Turkey and Central Asia in their new homeland. The growth in the number of intellectuals among them led one specialist on Xinjiang to write that "The most powerful impact on the emergence of a Uyghur national consciousness was generated by modern education."[1]

The Jadid movement, which developed among Muslims in Russia and emphasized Western-style modernization and education as the proper path for the Turkic people, influenced these intellectuals. Central Asian Turks, such as Ismail Gaspirali, advocated a transition from a traditional Islamic education toward a secular and modern education, a view that also spread among the émigrés from Xinjiang. Intellectuals were a vital force in the effort to create a Uyghur national identity. The educated elite would be the greatest advocates and popularizers of such an identity, pointing to a shared view of the past and emphasizing the history not only of the Turks, but also, via Islam, of their Arab and Iranian heritage. Despite the identification of many non-Han with their specific oases, intellectuals emphasized the larger Uyghur identity. When they returned to Xinjiang from Turkey and Russia, their creation of poetry, novels, and music also contributed to such a Uyghur identity. A recent study[2] suggests that the pilgrimages to shrines of saints were still another element in promoting Uyghur unity and identity. The *shaykhs*, who maintained the shrines, preserved written accounts, and told stories to pilgrims about a shared past, which strengthened the bonds of those championing the idea of a Uyghur people.

Nonetheless, in the early years of the Communist period, the Soviets did not perceive the Uyghurs as a national minority. In 1925, the Commission for the Study of the Tribal Composition of the Population of Russia did not accept them as a nationality.[3] Yet Soviet interest and involvement in the Uyghurs' homeland in Xinjiang accelerated in the late 1920s because the Chinese government, under Chiang Kai-shek and his Guomindang party, did not, as we have seen, control Xinjiang, offering the Soviets considerable opportunities for trade and cultural and political influence. Uyghurs from Xinjiang moved freely into Soviet Central Asia, where they sought employment and tended to be exploited.

It suited the Soviets to treat the Uyghurs as a national minority independent of China, based on a pamphlet by Joseph Stalin titled *Marxism and the National Question*. Stalin defined a nation as one with a "community of language, community of territory, and community of economic life" and "community of psychological makeup," and he inveighed against Great Russian chauvinism in dealing with national minorities. Yet, he also condemned local nationalism; the "nations" would have to accept rule by the Communists, the vanguard of the proletariat.[4] His work eventually provided the rationale for organizing a republic for each accepted nationality, though it would be ruled by the government of the USSR. The USSR identified various Turkic groups within its own borders as nations and thereby set the stage for the identification of the Uyghurs as a nation in Xinjiang as well. Thus, in the early 1930s, the term "Uyghur" began to be used for the largest contingent of non-Han in Xinjiang. The term led to greater identification among this group of Turkic peoples and to stirrings of greater unity beyond a specific town or oasis. Yet these Uyghurs, particularly intellectuals, did not accept the Stalinist dictum that they acquiesce to the Communists.

The founding of the Eastern Turkistan Islamic Republic in Kashgar, by a small group, in 1933 reflected the heightening of Uyghur national identity and the resistance to repression by Han warlords and merchants. The new Turkic leaders proclaimed their independence and emphasized a hybrid structure. They proposed devotion to Islam but also support for modern educational and medical systems. Because their government did not survive for long, it is difficult to determine what the leaders would have done. Would they have moved toward modernization? Or would they have focused on an Islamic state based on sharia or Islamic law? Would they have opted to shift from rule by a small group to more inclusive governance? Yet they faced severe financial problems as well as hostility from Chiang Kai-shek's government in Nanjing and rival Muslims in Xinjiang.

Ma Zhongying, leader of one of these rival groups, was a Chinese Muslim or Dungan from Northwest China who crushed the Eastern Turkistan Islamic Republic in 1934, resulting in a chaotic struggle for control. In brutal campaigns, Ma compelled some of the leaders of the republic to flee and subsequently occupied the critical and fabled city of Kashgar. For a time, Han, Hui (or Chinese Muslims), and Uyghur forces engaged in battles, with no definitive results. Chiang Kai-shek, who was based in Nanjing and thus a considerable distance from Xinjiang, was unable to be the decisive voice in selecting among the combatants and in achieving peace and stability.

USSR INVOLVEMENT AND CHINESE AND UYGHUR RESPONSES

The USSR played the critical role in the outcome. It eventually backed a Han military man named Sheng Shicai, who had been an underling in the Jin Shuren regime, as the new ruler of Xinjiang. Although the USSR's Joseph Stalin initially supported the Eastern Turkistan Islamic Republic, perhaps as a means of detaching the region from China, he ultimately turned against it for fear that it might inspire the neighboring Central Asian republics to break away from the USSR. Thus, he offered military assistance to Sheng and lured to the USSR or, depending on the source consulted, kidnapped Ma Zhongying, Sheng's major opponent, where he died or was executed.

The Soviets provided economic and technical assistance for Sheng's government. Russians streamed into Xinjiang to aid Sheng. Within a short time, Xinjiang had a greater trade turnover with the USSR than with China, and it seemed to be linking its future toward the West. When the Chinese Communists took power in 1949, they were concerned about the connections between Xinjiang and the USSR and have remained suspicious of Xinjiang's relations with the currently independent Central Asian countries. The peoples of Kazakhstan, Turkmenistan, Uzbekistan, and Kyrgyzstan are mostly Turkic and share a common religion and many social customs with the Uyghurs.

In any event, with aid from the USSR and tacit agreement from Chiang Kai-shek about Sheng's leadership, this military man was accepted as the governor of Xinjiang. Sheng dealt with opposition ruthlessly. He inveighed against so-called Japanese spies and Turkic nationalists and imprisoned or executed Uyghurs, other Muslims, and even Chinese dissenters. With USSR assistance, he crushed a rebellious force in 1937. Intellectuals and military commanders were the victims of this onslaught. Cordial relations with the USSR translated into cooperation with the Chinese Communists and recruitment of some of them, including Mao Zedong's brother, into his government. Adopting USSR policies, he distinguished among different ethnic groups, including the Uyghurs, Kazakhs, Hui, and other less numerous minorities. Such a listing naturally contributed to Uyghur identity and offered the Uyghurs somewhat more opportunities in government and the economy. Although Sheng did not know the local languages, he attracted some Uyghur support as the economy improved. Nonetheless, the USSR perhaps gained the most because it received access to Xinjiang's abundant natural resources for almost a decade.

The onset of World War II, and especially the German invasion of the USSR, upended relations in Xinjiang. Sheng assumed that the Nazis would defeat the USSR and that he could no longer count on its economic and technical assistance. He had, in any case, incurred sizable debts from the USSR in accepting Soviet aid, and breaking with his patrons would relieve the region of its and his monetary obligations. Thus, he turned to Chiang Kai-shek for aid and severed economic relations with the USSR. This break with the USSR alienated the peoples of northern Xinjiang, particularly the Kazakhs who depended on trade of their animals and animal products with their northern neighbor. Sheng's agreement with China also prompted him to remove, detain, and execute Chinese Communists in his administration, including Mao Zedong's brother. He became ever more dependent on Chiang and the Guomindang, but as the USSR began pushing the Nazi troops out of its territory, Sheng broached the subject of a resumption of relations with Stalin. The USSR no longer trusted Sheng and revealed his duplicity to the Guomindang, which recalled him from Xinjiang and took charge of the region, appointing Wu Zhongxin as the new governor in 1944.

After removing Sheng, the Guomindang instituted despised and oppressive policies that provoked considerable dissent. The new government persisted in pursuing Sheng's attempts to end Xinjiang's trade and technical relations with the USSR. Kazakh and other peoples in northern Xinjiang who depended on the USSR were alienated by this policy. In addition, corruption, mismanagement, and high taxes prompted the rise of what the Communists referred to as the Three Districts Revolution or the second Eastern Turkistan Republic in 1944. The districts of Yili, Tacheng, and Altay in northern Xinjiang challenged Chiang

Kai-shek's control. Osman Batur, a Kazakh leader often based in Mongolia, also sought initially to break away from Guomindang China, but eventually he supported the Guomindang against the Chinese Communists. Quite a number of Kazakhs had migrated to western Mongolia to flee from Tsarist Russia, and Osman Batur could thus use Mongolia as a base for his thrusts into Xinjiang. His campaigns and those of the Eastern Turkistan Republic propelled them into control of northern Xinjiang. With Guomindang forces unable to defeat the Eastern Turkistan Republic, Chiang Kai-shek sent a representative named Zhang Zhizhong to end the conflict.

With assistance from the USSR, by 1946, Zhang had devised a peace agreement with the Eastern Turkistan Republic, which also seemed to serve as the foundation for a Xinjiang government. Zhang would be the chairman of the government and would control the military. Yet the Uyghurs and other ethnic groups were granted positions in the government. Zhang acted to achieve stability and sought an evenhanded approach to both the Chinese and the Uyghurs, allowing Turkic cultural expression and education. He also permitted the USSR once again to engage in trade and to gain access to Xinjiang's mineral and natural resources, a vital objective for the Russians.

The appearance of a settlement between China and the Turkic population turned out to be deceptive. The Eastern Turkistan Republic maintained its own separate police and military forces in northern Xinjiang. The underlying problem was the status of the Turkic groups, particularly the Uyghurs in Xinjiang. Would they be granted autonomy, or would they seek independence? The Eastern Turkistan Republic, with support from the USSR, believed that the Guomindang had not treated the Uyghurs well. An ideological split also appeared, as the USSR emphasized the Uyghurs as a separate nationality, whereas the Guomindang, associated with Turkic leaders known as the Three Effendis, portrayed the people of Xinjiang as of Turkic, not Uyghur, backgrounds and claimed Xinjiang as part of China. The Three Effendis asserted that the USSR's use of such specific terms as Uyghurs, Kazakhs, and Kyrgyz was designed to sow divisions among the Turkic people and to prevent a unified front against outsiders. Under these circumstances, the Eastern Turkistan Republic, concerned about Guomindang involvement in Xinjiang, established a separate government in the city of Ghulja.

At the same time, Chiang Kai-shek, dissatisfied with Zhang Zhizhong's failure to prevent the rise of the Eastern Turkistan Republic, replaced him with one of the Three Effendis, Masūd Sabri, a Uyghur who would collaborate with the Guomindang and would allow Han leaders to dominate his government. The new regime reversed Zhang Zhizhong's policies, limiting the power and reducing the number of Uyghurs in government. The corruption that plagued the Guomindang in the central part of China also undermined Masūd Sabri's rule. Diverted by the civil war with the Chinese Communists, Chiang Kai-shek's government in Nanjing did not act until January of 1949, when it dismissed Masūd Sabri and appointed Burhan Shahidi, a Tatar originally born in the USSR, as the new governor. This step was too late, for within a few months the Guomindang abandoned the Chinese mainland and fled to Taiwan.

The second Eastern Turkistan Republic itself confronted difficulties. One was that the USSR supported it economically and with technical assistance. Its actual dependence on the USSR is difficult to gauge. To be sure, it needed the USSR's products and assistance, but it had its own objectives. The goals of different leaders diverged, which weakened them and exposed their vulnerability. Some mistrusted the USSR and sought to cooperate with the Guomindang, in hopes that it would become sensitive to their ethnicity. Others, especially in northern Xinjiang, had had a profitable trade with and received assistance from the USSR and were appalled by Guomindang corruption and oblivious to the maintenance of Turkic culture. They opted for a continued relationship with the USSR. Both sought considerable autonomy and perhaps even independence from China and the USSR.

The question that remains is whether ordinary Uyghur and other Turkic groups were aligned with their leaders. Were they more interested in economic relations with their two neighbors than in issues of autonomy or independence? Commerce with the USSR and even with Han merchants benefited northern Xinjiang's traders. An independent state, which some in the Eastern Turkistan Republic favored, might actually undermine this commerce.

CHINESE COMMUNISTS EMERGE VICTORIOUS

This conundrum became irrelevant as the Chinese Communists overwhelmed the Guomindang in late 1949 and took power in China, including Xinjiang. Burhan Shahidi, whom Chiang Kaishek had appointed governor in early 1949, was aware of the Guomindang's abandonment of more and more territory in the central part of China. He and Tao Zhiyue, the Chinese leader of the Guomindang army in Xinjiang, faced a dilemma, as the Chinese People's Liberation Army, the Communist military, occupied provinces in northwest China adjacent to Xinjiang. They could have challenged the People's Liberation Army, but they determined that that would be a fruitless policy that would result in numerous casualties. Despite Guomindang instructions to oppose the People's Liberation Army, Tao ignored these commands and instead informed the Chinese Communists that he would surrender. In light of later events, it is worth noting that Uyghurs guided the People's Liberation Army through the daunting Taklamakan desert. Some Uyghurs obviously thought that the Communists would be a good option for Xinjiang's Turkic population. The Chinese Communists might not be ideal, but the Uyghurs may have believed in Mao Zedong's assurances that minority cultures and languages would be protected and preserved under Communism. In any event, in the fall of 1949, the Chinese Communist commander Wang Zhen moved his troops into southern Xinjiang and became the Chinese Communist Party secretary in Xinjiang from 1950 to 1952.

At the same time, the Chinese Communists faced leaders in the Eastern Turkistan Republic government, in northern Xinjiang, whose allegiances were unclear. Economic relations with the USSR had prompted these leaders to adopt a positive attitude toward Communism, although their own philosophies and values did not necessarily jibe with that system. The Chinese Communists may also have been suspicious about their links with the USSR because of concern about Stalin's interest in bringing Xinjiang into the Soviet sphere of influence. Nonetheless, the Chinese Communists opened negotiations with the Eastern Turkistan leaders and in August of 1949 invited them to attend a meeting of the National People's Consultative Conference in Beijing. The Turkic leaders and a Han representative associated with them departed on a plane bound for Beijing, which did not reach its destination. A few months later, the Chinese discovered bits of the plane near Lake Baikal and proclaimed the crash an accident. Because the Eastern Turkistan Republic's major figures had not renounced a policy of independence, suspicions have arisen around this convenient accident. Rumors spread that the Chinese Communists shot down the plane.

Another theory that developed was that the USSR was the culprit because Stalin believed that the East Turkistan leaders would seek independence when they negotiated with the Chinese Communists, a threat to Soviet aspirations for influence in northern Xinjiang. Judging from later developments, USSR involvement appears unlikely, and the Chinese Communists' role is uncertain. Whatever happened, the Chinese Communists had more leverage in northern Xinjiang after the deaths of the Eastern Turkistan Republic leaders. The Chinese Communists then appointed Saifudin Azizi, a reliable supporter and a Uyghur who had been minister of education under the Eastern Turkistan Republic, as the representative to the National People's Consultative Conference, an important governmental body at that time. They were now assured that the Eastern Turkistan Republic was no longer a threat and that they had a great opportunity to add Xinjiang to their domains.

NEW COMMUNIST POLICIES

The PRC now had to develop policies for a region that constituted one-sixth of its territory and was blessed with considerable mineral and natural resources. Yet incorporation of Xinjiang was a mixed blessing, even in geographical terms. Although the north had abundant pasture and farmland, two-thirds of the region was composed of deserts and mountains, and the arable land was limited. Even more critical was the lack of water. Xinjiang's location was also problematic because it was closer to the USSR, and, in particular, the Central Asian republics, than to Beijing, and the population shared the language, religion, diet, and culture of the USSR's Central Asian peoples.

Xinjiang itself was riven with divisions. Such towns as Turfan in eastern Xinjiang had traded with the Han for centuries and had tolerably good relations with Han merchants. On the other hand, the Altishahr, which was composed of the cities of Kashgar, Khotan, Yarkand, Uch-Turfan, Aksu, and Yangyi Hisar and lay to the south and west, was not as integrated with China and had the largest non-Han populations. Khotan, which had been a Buddhist center in traditional times, maintained contacts with South Asia, and Kashgar had the closest association with Islam. Its Id Kah mosque was the main religious center and attracted numerous worshippers. The city also had hundreds of other smaller mosques. Yili, in northwestern Xinjiang, with its capital of Yining, possessed abundant pasture as well as arable land. It bordered on the Kazakh Republic of the USSR, and the Chinese Communists were concerned that Kazakhs inhabited both the USSR and their own territory in Yili. The potential for USSR claims or difficulties along the border could not be ruled out.

Xinjiang's ethnic diversity also would worry the PRC. Uyghurs were the dominant group, with a population of 4.87 million or 75 percent of the population as of the census conducted in 1953. The Han consisted of only 6 percent of Xinjiang's population. According to the views of some Uyghurs, the Uyghurs shared a common history, religion, diet, and culture, and their intellectuals could trace a common heritage through the Iranian epic, the *Shah Nameh*, and their Turkic histories. Shared novels, poems, music, festivals, language, and clothing also bound them as a distinct group. Their worship and pilgrimages to the shrines of religious dignitaries, their cemeteries adjacent to such shrines, their mullahs and mosques, and their *mahtabs* (or religious schools) and *mäshräps* (or social gatherings) all contributed to their religious identity.

Other specialists have challenged this view of Uyghur identity, noting a distinction between the rural and urban-based Uyghurs, and one anthropologist has asserted that Xinjiang's inhabitants identified with their native towns or oases and had only a limited identification with a larger Uyghur identity.[5] These scholars have argued that so-called Uyghurs were a more divided than unified group. Some were bitterly opposed to the Han and the PRC, but some sought an end to hostilities and hoped for the better life the Chinese Communists promised. These differing views would naturally influence PRC policy toward Xinjiang.

The other principal minorities were the Hui and the Kazakhs. Like the Uyghurs, the Hui were Muslims, but they were Chinese and did not conceive of establishing an independent state. The Hui had their own schools and mosques, which distinguished them from the Uyghurs. The Kazakhs, who had traditionally been pastoral nomads, resided principally in northern Xinjiang, and, as noted, had close connections with the USSR. Other and less numerous groups included the Shibo (or descendants of the Manchus), Mongols, Kyrgyz, and Tajiks (of Iranian heritage).

The multiethnic region of Xinjiang posed unique difficulties for the PRC. Most of the Xinjiang population was comprised of Muslims, which added to the problems for the Chinese Communists who professed to be atheists. The PRC thus needed to consider the effects of its policies in Xinjiang on the Islamic world. Because it did not wish to alienate the Muslim countries, it could not be viewed as suppressing Islam. The PRC had also annexed a region that had strong connections with the USSR. Although the PRC and the USSR had, in theory, a similar ideology, they had different and occasionally contentious objectives, which would shortly cause economic and territorial disputes. Xinjiang's relatively unmechanized economy, with farming, herding, and some limited mineral and natural resource extraction, did not jibe with the PRC's aspirations and its preference for a proletarian society. The industrial working class was tiny.

Xinjiang's economy and society also posed significant problems. Life in Xinjiang was extraordinarily difficult. A. Doak Barnett, the eminent specialist on modern China, started his career with an extended trip through various regions of China from 1947 to 1949 and spent September of 1948 in Xinjiang. He observed:

> A considerable amount of land that either is not cultivated or could be cultivated even more intensively . . . very little exploitation even of known resources in the province . . . [v]irtually no industrialization has yet taken place . . . [s]inkiang [Xinjiang] is a "backward" and undeveloped area . . . modern transport is totally lacking. There is not a single railway . . . [n]epotism, graft, corruption, and even violence were recurring phenomena . . . [f]inancial reform has not yet been accomplished . . . [t]here are only about 20 hospitals, not one of which is really modern . . . there are still only 15 middle schools in the whole province, and the one institution of higher learning, the Sinkiang College [later to be Xinjiang University], is rather a joke.[6]

Many non-Han barely eked out an existence, as poverty engulfed most of Xinjiang's inhabitants. Women, in particular, led difficult lives and had few political, social, and economic rights. Their roles in Islamic rituals were curtailed. As in many areas of China, parents arranged marriages, and drudgery characterized most women's lives. Thus, the traditional Uyghur economy, society, and culture in Xinjiang were in parlous condition.

Another problem for the PRC was that it had to contend with non-Han who had departed from China either earlier in the twentieth century or after the Communist victory. The largest group of Uyghurs was in the Kazakh Soviet Socialist Republic, and another smaller group was found in the other Central Asian Soviet Republics. In addition, thousands of Kazakhs and Uyghurs had fled before the Communist takeover in 1949, trekked through the Himalayas, and reached India in the early 1950s. Once they had arrived in India, a few leaders inquired about a Central Intelligence Agency operative who had apparently made promises of support for the Uyghurs. They learned, to their disappointment, that he had been killed in Tibet in 1950. Unlike the Tibetans who left China after a revolt in 1959, the non-Han did not intend to remain in India. Those Han who had been leaders in Xinjiang such as Sheng Shicai moved to Taiwan with Chiang Kai-shek, whose government was eager to attract non-Han officials to Taiwan to legitimize its claims to Xinjiang. In this case, Mao and Chiang agreed, as both insisted that Xinjiang was part of China. Yolbars Khan (1889–1981), a Uyghur who had fought against the Chinese Communists, fled to South Asia but then went to Taiwan and represented the group who accepted Chinese suzerainty over Xinjiang. He tried repeatedly but unsuccessfully to convince other non-Han leaders to join him in Taiwan. Appreciating his efforts and using him to justify Chinese claims, Chiang Kai-shek appointed him governor of Xinjiang.[7]

Many of the non-Han who rejected calls from Yolbars had actually settled in Turkey under the leadership of Isa Yusuf Alptekin, who sought an independent Turkestan and opposed rule by either Mao Zedong or Chiang Kai-shek, and smaller groups migrated to other European and Asian countries and the United States. The two principal diasporas in Taiwan and Turkey could not unite, a prelude to repeated divisions among these groups. Yet, as we will note, a few of these expatriates would, in the future, be successful in shaping foreigners' perceptions of China's policies in Xinjiang. At this time, however, the PRC focused on ruling Xinjiang itself, not on the diaspora.

The first step for the PRC was to defuse tensions over border issues in Mongolia and Xinjiang. It is no accident that the first of Mao Zedong's only two trips abroad was to the USSR. In December of 1949 and January of 1950, he traveled to Moscow to negotiate with Joseph Stalin and other Soviet leaders to produce agreements concerning the Sino-Soviet relationship. He was determined to achieve stability on the Xinjiang border and to restrict Soviet influence and trade. Needing Soviet economic and technical assistance, Mao was compelled to abandon claims to Mongolia, but he protected China's governance over Xinjiang. Again, it was no accident that his entourage included the Uyghur Saifudin Azizi because Mao clearly intended to bolster China's jurisdiction over Xinjiang and needed a representative of the ethnic minority to do so.

Once these negotiations had concluded, Mao began to implement his professed policies concerning the ethnic minorities. He portrayed himself as the liberator of the oppressed minorities. As early as 1938 and perhaps even earlier, he had spoken about the minority ethnic groups (*shaoshu minzu*). He did not depict them as independent nationalities but as an ethnic group within China. Emphasizing that the minorities had equal rights with the Han, he also proclaimed that they had the right to handle their own affairs and to choose committees to cooperate with Han committees in determining economic and political policies in their regions. He admonished officials to respect the minorities' cultures, customs, and religions; to prevent any expressions of contempt toward the non-Han; to abandon Han chauvinism; and to avoid compelling the various ethnic groups to use the Chinese spoken and written languages. A meeting of the Chinese People's Consultative Conference in September of 1949 had already presented these views in its published Common Program. The participants pledged to protect the minorities' languages, traditions, and religions and to establish a system of regional autonomy. Yet the Consultative Conference also warned the minorities to steer clear of "nationalism and chauvinism." Despite this one discordant note, most of the message was positive. The Chinese Communists promised not to interfere in their ethnic minorities' societies.

Mao originally assumed that the minorities would gradually assimilate into Chinese society, and the Communists would label this view as *ronghe* or fusion of Han and non-Han, in particular, through intermarriages. Thus, he ordered officials to pursue flexible policies that would not antagonize the Uyghurs or other ethnic groups. In his view, the minorities would naturally be Sinicized through intermarriage or through strong identification with Han culture. Mao's view did not jibe with the reality concerning intermarriage. As he traveled through Xinjiang in 1948, A. Doak Barnett noted, "The Muslims are extremely sensitive about marriage of their daughters to infidels . . . even respectable marriage frequently enrages the sensitive Muslims, particularly the Uighurs."[8] Many other observers have described the same attitudes toward intermarriage, and in recent discussions with Uyghurs and Han in the United States and Xinjiang, I received the same message.

The military and the officials appointed in Xinjiang did not always abide by Mao's gradualist approach. Wang Zhen, the initial Han commander and Communist Party secretary, arrested and, in some cases, executed the remaining leaders of the Eastern Turkistan Republic. In 1951, he also captured and killed the Kazakh leader, Osman Batur. As the chief military man in Xinjiang, he maintained control for two years and temporized on establishing a regular government. Soviet influence over commerce and technical assistance and minor outbreaks by minority groups prompted the stationing of his troops in the region. The central government could not fund this large force, and these troops would need to be self-sustaining.

The PRC eventually organized the Production Construction Military Corps (or PCC, familiarly known as the *bingtuan*) to provide the wherewithal for the former soldiers residing in Xinjiang whom the state could not support. The *bingtuan* would now serve as a militia and enforcers of law and order (even having its own prisons) but would also be involved in such infrastructure projects as building dams and developing irrigation complexes. Its members would set about farming and would eventually reclaim quite a bit of land. As the economy developed, the *bingtuan* would assume nonagricultural responsibilities. The PRC was motivated to have a militia force both to ensure Han control and to prevent the USSR from exerting considerable influence in Xinjiang. Mao's assumption that assimilation would resolve hostilities led to a policy of compelling some Han to move to Xinjiang, and the *bingtuan* often served to acclimate such migrants to their new homeland and to incorporate them in the economy.

Having chosen to use the *bingtuan* for security, for economic reform, and for orientation of Han migrants, Xinjiang's leaders started to deal with cultural issues. Policies regarding Islam were crucial. In July of 1952, Burhan and Saifudin, leaders in Xinjiang, met with other Muslims in Beijing and founded the Chinese Islamic Association, with Burhan as its president. The professed aims of the organization were to educate Muslims about religious issues within the sphere of "social development," to guide academic research about Islam, to facilitate travel on the hajj or pilgrimage to Mecca, to promote exchanges with Islamic countries, to manage Islamic law within the context of Chinese law, and to foster community service and philanthropy through the mosques. Other important and more government-controlled tasks included training Islamic teachers, ensuring love of the motherland and support of socialism, and correcting ideas about Islam. The establishment of the Chinese Islamic Association signified government supervision and control over the Islamic leadership. All religious dignitaries had to register with the association and confirm their allegiance to the PRC and to its social and economic systems. The association kept tabs on the mullahs and other religious leaders and would not tolerate antiparty views. Yet the PRC and the local authorities did not, at this time, ban services at mosques, nor did the central government meddle extensively concerning Islamic customs and practices, though local Han officials supervised religious services.

The PRC did initiate policies on what it perceived to be secular concerns. *Qadis* (or judges) who interpreted Islamic laws would no longer be arbiters in legal conflicts. Communist cadres would have authority on minor matters, and government-appointed judges would adjudicate major conflicts. Communist law took precedence over traditional Islamic law. In addition, mosques lost much of their endowments (or *waqfs*), especially in the form of land, that wealthy and devout Muslims had donated to them. The state would often provide the pay of religious leaders. Shrines lost much of their funding; the *shaykhs* who administered them lost their positions, and many of the texts in their possession disappeared. Many shrines closed, and renowned ones would be turned into tourist attractions. Mosques had fewer resources, and the PRC, in what it termed land reform, turned over land formerly owned by mosques as private property to farmers, so that ordinary Uyghurs and other non-Han and the new Han migrants to Xinjiang profited by receiving individual plots.

Gradualism was the pattern, as the government did not immediately communize the land. Instead, it initially confiscated land that religious institutions and landlords owned and turned it over to poor peasants. The authorities sought, in this way, to ingratiate themselves to the Uyghurs, Kazakhs, and other non-Han in Xinjiang, and at the same time to deflect concerns about the policy of promoting Han migration into the region. The government moved Han into the area, a policy that generated the most hostility from the non-Han peoples. Despite the possibility of such enmity, the leaders believed that the Han and the Uyghurs and the Kazakhs would eventually intermarry. Their hopes turned out to be unrealistic. The rate of intermarriage would remain low.

This failure was due, in part, to the stereotypes each held of the other. Some Han mocked the Uyghurs for eating with their hands and were uncomfortable with Muslim practices, dress, and diet, especially the Islamic aversion to consumption of pork. Other Han went further and perceived the Uyghurs to be dim, lazy, and backward. Some Uyghurs portrayed the Han as unclean and smelling of spices. Many on both sides found the other slippery in mercantile transactions. By and large, the two groups did not socialize, limiting the opportunities for intermarriage.

Overcoming these difficulties and promoting the assimilation of the Uyghurs would not be an easy task for Xinjiang's leaders, but they also faced other problems. Like the leadership in Beijing, they were concerned about the rest of the Islamic world's views regarding their policies in Xinjiang. In the early 1950s, the PRC, the government of China, which the United States and some other Western countries had not recognized, attempted to establish harmonious relations with Islamic lands in the Middle East and South and Southeast Asia. New leaders, including Gamal Abdel Nasser in Egypt and Sukarno in Indonesia, had come to power in what came to be called the Third World, neutral countries in the Cold War between the United States and its allies and the Communist nations. With scant recognition and support beyond the Communist bloc, the PRC sought legitimacy through acceptance by Third World countries, many of which had Muslim populations. It did not wish to be perceived as suppressing Islam either in Xinjiang or, in fact, throughout the country. In 1955, Zhou Enlai, the premier and the foreign minister of the PRC, deliberately attended the well-known Bandung Conference of Asian and African nations, which included a number of Islamic states, to ingratiate China with the Third World lands. In sum, the PRC could not afford to target Islam other than a general advocacy of atheism.

By 1954, the Xinjiang leaders had achieved many of their goals, except for the establishment of a government. They had pressed forward with so-called land reform, which entailed expropriation of land from mosques, *waqfs*, and wealthy landlords and converted it into private property for poor peasants. In the process, they had engaged in a "Red Terror," executing landlords and others they deemed obstreperous. The *bingtuan*, which had initially consisted of PLA soldiers, had increased to about 750,000 and founded state farms and served as a preparatory force for development of mineral resources and for establishment of industries. The long-range plan was to extract taxes from agriculture to provide capital for industrialization. The PRC encouraged and mostly compelled Han from central China to migrate to Xinjiang to secure the border with the USSR, to serve as a labor force, and to reduce the influence of the Uyghurs and other non-Han peoples.

Having achieved what the PRC perceived to be a relatively stable economy, it needed to devise a governmental system for Xinjiang. A comprehensive study listed numerous so-called minority nationalities, including the Han, and Xinjiang had representatives of thirteen of these groups, including the Han, Kazakhs, Uyghurs, Kyrgyz, Hui, Tajiks, and Sibo (or Manchu speakers). Save for the Uyghurs and the Han, the regions with the largest concentrations of these minorities, the Kazakhs and the Kyrgyz, were granted such autonomous subdivisions as prefectures, districts, or counties, depending on population size. Such groupings bolstered the individual minorities and served to separate them from the Uyghurs, the most populous group. In 1955, the PRC offered official recognition to the Uyghurs as the largest constituent of the population by settling on the Xinjiang Uyghur Autonomous Region (XUAR) as the designated name for the area. However, autonomy was limited. Although the governor was the Uyghur Saifudin, Wang Enmao, a lieutenant general in the People's Liberation Army who had replaced Wang Zhen as the secretary of the Communist Party in Xinjiang in 1952, the PRC authorities in Beijing were the real policy makers.

Slightly before the founding of the XUAR, the leaders had been promoting development of agricultural producers' cooperatives. This policy had started in other parts of China and had faced some opposition, but the hostility in Xinjiang was greater. Mutual aid teams had taken hold in Xinjiang, but the cooperatives had scarcely made a dent. Moreover, the pastoral peoples in northern Xinjiang had also resisted cooperatives. By 1955 a few had joined, but over the next couple of years a government propaganda campaign, emphasizing the cooperatives' social, medical, and educational benefits, bore fruit. These benefits were, in fact, tangible. Medical services, including everything from basically trained medical personnel to clinics to hospitals, introduced modern medicine. Elementary and secondary schools were founded, and Xinjiang College was bolstered and improved and became the comprehensive Xinjiang University.

These policies were implemented gradually and did not generate much overt opposition. Major violent episodes did not erupt. One of the principal non-Han people's complaints centered on the arrival of so many Han settlers, who also frequently received good jobs. If their numbers increased, the possibility that the Han would outnumber the indigenous population was a growing concern. Another concern was the lack of real autonomy, with power principally in the hands of Han Communist cadres. Yet better medical and educational facilities and inclusive welfare programs initially compensated for the possible cultural and economic threats and the lack of political power.

REPEATED CHANGES IN COMMUNIST POLICIES

Cataclysmic events in the Communist world would shatter the relative peace and stability in Xinjiang. In February of 1956, Nikita Khrushchev, the first secretary of the Communist Party of the USSR, presented a speech titled "The Cult of Personality and Its Consequences," which was a blistering critique of Joseph Stalin and the purges and other damage the Soviet leader had inflicted on the country. Within a few months, the Soviet bloc in Eastern Europe exploded, with demonstrations and protests in Poland and a revolution in Hungary. Khrushchev's anti-Stalin speech and the Eastern Europeans' desire for greater independence from the USSR revealed cracks in the Soviet bloc. The violence shocked the PRC leaders, especially Mao.

Concerned about the spread of such violent dissent, Mao sought to get ahead of such expressions of discontent before it got out of hand. In late 1956 and early 1957, he initiated a Hundred Flowers campaign, which referred to the Warring States period (475–221 BCE), when Confucianism, Daoism, and other so-called Flowers, or philosophies, competed for primacy in China. In a speech "On the Correct Handling of the Contradictions Among the People," Mao encouraged criticism of the Communist Party, both to free bottled-up hostility and to identify dissenters. Some have suggested that the Hundred Flowers campaign was actually a ploy to lure the most vociferous and perhaps bitterest opponents of the PRC into revealing themselves. Whatever the motivations, Mao and the government were apparently startled by the number and intensity of the critiques. By May, Mao ended the Hundred Flowers campaign and initiated an anti-Rightist Rectification campaign, proclaiming that the critics, over the past three months, were dangerous antigovernment agents. The new campaign resulted in the arrest and imprisonment at Gulag-like locations of leading intellectuals who had been ardent critics of the Communist Party and the PRC.

The Hundred Flowers and the anti-Rightist Rectification campaigns initiated more radical policies in Xinjiang. Non-Han criticism during the Hundred Flowers campaign in Xinjiang was based, in part, on ethnic issues, and Han migrants who had been compelled to move to the region added to the critiques. The native inhabitants often complained that the autonomy that they had been promised was a mirage. Han Communist cadres dominated the most important political and economic positions and often ignored or adopted a condescending attitude toward non-Han leaders. They overrode the powers of Saifudin and other "minority" officials. The State Council in Beijing could overrule the local People's Congresses and did not permit an independent judiciary. The central government determined the most significant policies and controlled the extraction of natural resources, which was vital in Xinjiang. To be sure, some non-Han officials had positions in government, but Han personnel almost always had the most important responsibilities.

These criticisms in Xinjiang bothered Mao and his associates. They believed that their policies had benefited the population by improving the educational and medical systems and by offering land to poor peasants and animals to poor herders. The government was also irritated by the Han migrants who criticized Communist policies because they had been forced to leave their native provinces and to resettle in Xinjiang. As in the central part of China, some Han and non-Han critics were arrested or purged from their positions.

EMERGENCE OF RADICAL INITIATIVES

The more radical policies that developed after the Hundred Flowers and the anti-Rightist Rectification campaigns were due, in part, to relations with the USSR and the desire for more rapid economic growth. Although the PRC and the USSR shared a Communist ideology, tensions between them lay just beneath the surface. In the 1920s and 1930s, Stalin had not always supported the Chinese Communists in their struggles with Chiang Kai-shek; and, on several occasions, he instructed them to join in a united front with Chiang's Guomindang party. Disputes about territory, ideology, and tactics, especially regarding relations with the Western capitalist countries, had flared up ever since. Mao resented the condescending attitude of the Soviets toward China and their depiction of themselves as the Big Brothers and the Chinese as the Younger Brothers.

The Sino-Soviet relationship in Xinjiang was particularly tense. Ever since the Russian Revolution, the Soviets had been heavily involved in the region. They had invested in mineral resource sites, traded with local inhabitants, and dispatched technical advisers to assist in economic development. They had also supported rulers and specific government policies. The PRC feared that the Soviets would dominate and perhaps would even seek to displace China in Xinjiang. It was also concerned that the Kazakhs and other minorities who had connections with Kazakhs or other Turkic peoples across the Soviet border would opt to live in the USSR. However, when the Communists took power in 1949, they had to accommodate to the USSR because they needed funds and technical assistance. In the early 1950s, the USSR provided loans in return for Xinjiang's natural resources, via joint stock companies, but the PRC was eager to rid itself of these companies in order to limit Soviet involvement.

Nikita Khrushchev's rise to power in 1954 exacerbated the PRC's suspicions. The Soviet leader fostered better relations with the Western countries through a so-called thaw and had personally criticized Stalin and his cult of personality. The PRC distrusted the West and was appalled by Khrushchev's policy of peaceful coexistence with the United States and other capitalist countries. Territorial disputes, ideological differences, and differing economic strategies led to the beginnings of a Sino-Soviet split. In 1958, Khrushchev's reaction to the PRC's battles with Taiwan and the United States over control of Quemoy and Matsu, two islands off the east coast of China, contributed to further animosity between the two Communist countries. When Khrushchev refused to help China and sent his minister of foreign affairs, Andrei Gromyko, to urge caution concerning this territorial dispute, Mao began to suspect that the USSR would not come to China's assistance in case of conflict with the United States. An isolated China would have to depend on itself alone. By the late 1950s, a full-scale Sino-Soviet split was evident, with each side leveling harsh criticism of the other.

In 1958, Mao, believing that he was in a corner, announced plans to make an unconventional increase in the rate of economic growth, via the so-called Great Leap Forward, in order to catch up with the great powers—the United States, the USSR, and other countries in the West. His plan entailed rapid economic growth not through technology but via labor, which was in abundant supply in China. Workers would construct dams or devise irrigation projects, mostly with their own hands rather than with equipment. The government even encouraged the creation of backyard furnaces to produce steel, which turned out to be a foolhardy project, as most of what was produced was not of sufficient quality and had to be discarded. A vital feature of the plan was an increase in agricultural production, which would provide the revenues for industrial development. Mao supported the establishment of communes, which would eliminate private property as much as possible. Under his scheme, peasants would receive wages rather than income from land they previously owned. In Communist terminology, peasants would become semi-proletarians. The communes would, in theory, be more efficient than private landholdings. Planting could be on a large scale, and mechanization would be facilitated. Commune creches and schools, as well as communal mess halls, would free women from baby and child care and domestic pursuits to join the labor force. Propaganda stressed hard work, which sometimes translated into extraordinary overtime labor, as the means to overtake most of the world's economies, except the United States and USSR, which were the two leading economies.

The emphasis on the tremendous increase in production placed great pressure on local leaders who, on occasion, responded by inflating the figures for actual harvests. They then used the excess of the allegedly bountiful harvests to pay taxes to the government, which exported the grains and other agricultural products to the USSR and the Eastern European Communist countries, partly to repay loans and partly to purchase machinery and other goods. This disastrous ploy led to significant food shortages in many rural areas. The imposition of Communist Party cadres as directors of some of the communes added to chaotic conditions. With limited experience in farming, they sometimes overruled knowledgeable peasants and ordered them, for example, to plant such export crops as tea in lands unsuited for such cultivation. They ingratiated themselves with their superiors by emphasizing cash crops, but they further depleted the food supply. Starvation and famine followed in the wake of these policies. Refugees who fled during this period described harrowing scenes of peasants who had labored all day on farms and in small factories then struggling to find scraps of food and eating rats and even tree bark. The Communist policy of sending students to work in the countryside (a policy known as *xiafang*), presumably to learn from the peasants but also to provide labor for infrastructure projects, exacerbated these difficulties. The students resented the policy, were not skilled in farming, and constituted another group that had to be fed.

Chaos also afflicted the communes in Xinjiang. The poor decision making of the central government and the commune directors harmed agricultural and pastoral economies. Starvation and famines struck, as in the rest of China. Statistics on deaths are difficult to come by, which is made even more complicated because some Han left the region and departed to cities or provinces in the central part of China in order to survive. Ethnic and religious issues created even more difficulties. Despite the parlous economic conditions, Han continued to migrate to Xinjiang. Some joined the *bingtuan*, others headed for the capital in Urumchi, which increasingly became a Han city; and still others who were accustomed to working in agriculture started to plant crops and set up farms on land formerly used for pasture in northern Xinjiang.

Another irritation in relations was the lack of flexibility concerning Islam and its practices. The PRC began to blame religious proscriptions on the limited progress in relations between Han and non-Han, including possible intermarriages or at least growing assimilation. It started to view Islam as a stumbling block in its policies in Xinjiang. Earlier, it had confiscated *waqfs*, land, and other property owned by the mosques, madrassas (or theological schools), and *mazars* (or shrines to prominent religious dignitaries of the past), which had provided income for philanthropy, social services, maintenance of the buildings, and the personal lifestyles of the religious leaders. The state had often turned over the land to poor peasants, which it hoped would ingratiate it with that part of the population. The government now decided that stronger measures were needed. It mandated stricter supervision over the mosques and shrines, prohibited pilgrimages to Mecca, and increased antireligious propaganda. This new policy somewhat undermined the earlier good feelings generated by providing confiscated land to the poor peasants.

Northern Xinjiang witnessed the most damaging and serious repercussions of the dramatic Great Leap Forward policies. The government had developed two programs that provoked protests from the Kazakhs and other groups in the north. One trend was to encourage even more Han settlers, who were mostly peasants, to migrate to the area. The settlers reverted to their expertise and carved out pastureland and converted it to farmland, alienating the herders who had occupied much of the region and, on occasion, damaging the earth. A second development was a more sustained attempt to communize the herding economy. Communes rather than individual herders would own the animals, and a herder would receive a wage rather than income based on work with his or her own herds. In the mid-1950s, the Mongolian People's Republic had just succeeded in its campaign to establish *negdels*, or cooperatives for the country's herders, but the Mongolian government had devoted considerable time and effort to explain the economic, social, medical, and educational benefits of the *negdels*. The authorities had not devoted the same kind of propaganda effort in Xinjiang.

By contrast, mostly Han cadres, in northern Xinjiang, had sped up the campaign for communes in the same frenzied manner as with other aspects of the Great Leap Forward. The herders were concerned that the communes limited their semiannual or even more frequent migrations to find water and grass for their animals in new locations. Such restrictions on their movements would, from their standpoint, disrupt their society. In addition, the herders could not rely on pasturage alone if they remained in one location because their animals would readily consume the nearby grasslands, which would perhaps even lead to desertification of the area. The PRC justified such limitations on movement by noting that the herders would have greater access to medical facilities, schools for their children, and other social benefits in remaining in one or two locations. Finally, northern Xinjiang had also been afflicted with the same problems as other parts of China during the Great Leap Forward. Statistics about production were inflated, precious goods were slated for export, and the ensuing lack of food led to starvation and famine.

This precipitous campaign of communization of the herds and the general chaotic conditions of the Great Leap Forward prompted a predictable response on the part of some Kazakhs and other groups in northern Xinjiang. In 1962, at least 60,000 and perhaps up to 100,000 of them fled to the USSR. The PRC quickly blamed Soviet propaganda for enticing these migrants, which exacerbated the Sino-Soviet split. Most of the escapees were Kazakh herders, but some were Uyghurs and Hui in a variety of occupations. This voluntary migration was a public relations catastrophe for the PRC government, as it took place in the midst of the ideological and territorial contretemps between China and the USSR. Part of the reason for the Great Leap Forward was to limit the influence of the USSR in Xinjiang. Rejection by a significant minority in China was a blow to the PRC's image and a public relations victory for the USSR. Another indication of the vitriol that divided the PRC and the USSR had taken place two years earlier, when the four years' experiment to employ Cyrillic for the Uyghur language ended and Latin temporarily replaced Cyrillic. The government responded to the immediate crisis of the non-Han emigration to the USSR by closing the border, stationing mostly Han troops there, and dismissing a few non-Han officials accused of abetting migrants.

Other events in southwest China contributed to disarray in the PRC. In 1959, a Tibetan rebellion, with support from the US's Central Intelligence Agency, flared up. PRC troops quickly suppressed it. Like the non-Han groups who fled to the USSR in 1962, Tibetan lay people and monks, prominently the Dalai Lama, crossed into India and established their own community in their new location. Mao Zedong, who had advocated a relatively moderate policy in Tibet and had not targeted the Dalai Lama, now believed that he could no longer trust the leader of the Tibetan Buddhists and thus initiated a harsher policy in Tibet.

At the same time, China's relations with the Mongolian People's Republic in the north deteriorated dramatically during the Great Leap Forward. Mao had recognized Mongolia's independence in 1950, after considerable pressure from Stalin. This set the stage for cordial Sino-Mongolian relations. The PRC sent Chinese laborers and technical experts to Mongolia to promote manufacturing and to construct apartments, roads, cultural centers, and the parliament building. For three decades before China and Mongolia initiated relations, the USSR had been Mongolia's closest ally and greatest trading partner and provider of aid. Once the Sino-Soviet split became apparent, Mongolia had to choose between its two partners or allies. Its lengthier relationship with the USSR, its closer links with Russian universities and technical institutes, its adoption of the Cyrillic alphabet for the Mongolian language, and the greater economic benefits associated with the USSR facilitated its selection. Mongolia began to expel the Chinese laborers and engineers, and by 1964, economic relations between the two countries had been severed.

In 1962, facing all these crises—isolation from the rest of the world, famine, poor economic results, and tense relations with the non-Han in Xinjiang—due to the radical Great Leap Forward, PRC leaders sought a moderate and less chaotic policy. Because Mao had been the principal architect of the Great Leap Forward, he would be relegated to a lower position in decision making for the next three or four years. The new leaders focused on a more rational economic policy, including modification of the communes and allowance of private property in land and animals. Economic recovery and provision of an adequate food supply were essential, and in Xinjiang, translated not only into more economic flexibility for peasants and herders, but also into fewer restrictions on Islam. The more moderate leaders, who included Liu Shaoqi, the chair of the PRC and the vice chair of the Communist Party, must have recognized that campaigns attacking Islam were counterproductive. Indeed, such policies did not jibe with Marxist thought that religion is part of the superstructure and would disappear of its own accord once social classes eroded and gave way. Direct attacks on and confrontations with religions were suspended. Thus, anti-Islamic propaganda and actions were suspended for four years.

Economic recovery and abandonment of the frenzied pace of the Great Leap Forward were the main policy objectives of the years from 1962 to 1966. In Xinjiang, the economy took precedence over political agendas and religion. Reports about starvation or famine rarely appeared; the backyard steel furnaces were no longer operating; recruitment of masses of laborers and a concomitant denigration of technology for hastily built infrastructure projects were abandoned. During this period, the Xinjiang government exerted less pressure on the peasants and herders to join collectives or communes, lightened the restrictions on Islam, limited the opposition to undertaking the hajj to Mecca and to pilgrimages to shrines, and began to follow a methodical approach to economic growth. Harassment of moderates ended, as did damage to property and incessant, frenzied, and vituperative propaganda about a Great Leap Forward. Rational economic development policies led to the completion of a railroad line to Urumchi, the capital of Xinjiang, creating greater links to the rest of China, and the beginnings of cotton cultivation in the region.

The main point of friction was Han in-migration. In 1953, the Uyghurs constituted 75 percent of the almost 4.87 million population and the Han only 6 percent. In the 1964 census, 54 percent of the population was Uyghur while the Han had increased dramatically to 33 percent of the total of 7.44 million. Nonetheless, the excesses of the Great Leap had receded, and the economy had grown from 1962 to 1966.

This relative calm ended when Mao swam in the Yangtze River in 1966. He announced, in this way, his vigor, his return to politics, and his support of radical policies. Excoriating some moderates as "capitalist roaders" and believing that revolutionary ardor needed to be restored, he encouraged attacks on entrenched bureaucrats and intellectuals. What he dubbed the Great Proletarian Cultural Revolution reverted to concerns about ideology and political purity rather than economic development. The ensuing disruptions testified to the primacy of politics because the economy was devastated. Schools and universities closed for a time, allowing young people to form so-called Red Guards who roamed around the country terrorizing anyone accused of harboring foreign views or even playing foreign music or representing traditional ideas. The Red Guards mocked, detained, injured, and even killed these so-called miscreants. Through the Red Guards, Mao punished those who had pushed him aside after the Great Leap Forward and anyone who did not support his radical approach, including Liu Shaoqi and Deng Xiaoping, who had taken charge of the economy after the failures of the Great Leap Forward and introduced more pragmatic policies, which Mao condemned as capitalist. Within a year, however, the Red Guards had created so much chaos that Mao was compelled to call upon the army to restrain them. Battles erupted, on occasion, between the two until the Red Guards were brought under control.

China's increasing isolation and lack of allies among the great powers accompanied and may have precipitated the Cultural Revolution. The Sino-Soviet split had heated up throughout the 1960s; and, at the same time, the United States had stationed half a million troops in Vietnam, a site not far from China. Paranoia or legitimate fears may have provoked extremes in policies. Mao's extremist views certainly helped him overwhelm his rivals and opponents, but they also set back China's economy, society, and culture. All suffered from the attacks on foreign ideas, music, literature, and anything smacking of traditional ideas.

The Cultural Revolution in Xinjiang was no doubt harmful. The Red Guards vented their fury on Wang Enmao, who had been the dominant figure in the Communist Party and the government in Xinjiang from 1952, although the Uyghur Saifudin held the mostly ceremonial position of the chair of the government. Wang responded by supporting the establishment of another Red Guard group, ushering in a period of conflict among a variety of different forces. Like other areas in China, Xinjiang was bedeviled with armed warfare, leading to numerous deaths. The various groups included not only the Red Guards, the *bingtuan*, and the military, but also divisions within each. A radical replaced Wang Enmao as leader of the Xinjiang Uyghur Autonomous Region and pressed for the Great Leap Forward's objective of communization of the land and the herds and labeled his opponents as "capitalist roaders." These chaotic conditions also resulted in a decline in both the herding and agricultural economies.

Such developments also influenced policies toward the non-Chinese peoples and Islam. The Red Guards portrayed the Uyghurs and other non-Han groups in Xinjiang as betrayers of the Revolution; and PRC officials, who had earlier opted to praise the principle of autonomy, were now concerned that few Han and non-Han had intermarried, a perennial issue. Assuming that the non-Han would have assimilated more rapidly after so many years of Communist rule, they now began to reexamine the policy of autonomy. Having witnessed considerable non-Han opposition during the Great Leap Forward, they started to criticize the non-Han. Their criticism began to include Islam because they believed that religious leaders were intransigent, preventing harmonious relations with the Han and even subverting the government.

Thus, they unleashed a propaganda campaign directed against Islam and started to reduce opportunities for Muslims to take part in the hajj or pilgrimage to Mecca. Perhaps taking their lead from the government, the Red Guards engaged in numerous attacks on Islam, destroying or damaging mosques, shrines, theological schools, copies of the Koran, and criticizing and manhandling religious leaders. Muslims could not practice their rituals without hindrance. Such impediments provoked Muslim hostility and undermined stability in Xinjiang. Instability and chaos did not serve to ingratiate the PRC with the non-Han and even the Han in Xinjiang.

The height of the Cultural Revolution lasted from 1966 to 1969, but it continued in modified form until the death of Mao in September of 1976. After 1969, the radical policies began to weaken. Events leading up to US President Richard Nixon's visit to China in 1972 testified to changes and a greater engagement with the world. Some PRC leaders recognized the need for rational planning for the economy and a reversal of the chaotic policies of the Cultural Revolution. They wanted to set the stage for changes, and Mao's death in 1976 and the imprisonment of Mao's wife, Jiang Qing, and her associates, known as the Gang of Four, offered them an opportunity to introduce new directions in the economy, politics, and society. By 1978, Deng Xiaoping, one of Mao's comrades in arms who had split with Mao, the so-called Great Helmsman, reemerged and returned to power after exile and promoted a different direction in which the economy prevailed over ideology and politics.

Some of the Uyghurs, on their side, complained that the Han were intent on destroying their way of life. They asserted that the Cultural Revolution's propaganda and actions against Islam and Uyghur traditions and practices, including clothing, music, and literature, were designed to subvert their cultural and ethnic identity. The government's lack of concern for the Muslim diet disturbed them as well. They complained that local officials during the Cultural Revolution compelled them to raise pigs, a taboo in Islam. Government changes in the transcription of the Uyghur language also irritated them. In the early 1950s, the Soviet influence had prompted the PRC to substitute the Cyrillic alphabet for the Arabic script for Uyghur, but the onset of the Sino-Soviet split led them in 1958 to substitute a Latin script for Cyrillic. Fervent Muslims accused the government in both cases of seeking to undermine their connection with the Arabic of the Koran and their Islamic faith. Some Uyghurs also objected to the Han stereotypes portraying them as lazy and afflicted with alcohol and drug problems. They believed that the Han denigrated their lifestyles.

Environmental and economic issues also concerned the Uyghurs. The government's main nuclear testing site was in Lop Nor in Xinjiang, which had led to an increase in the rate of cancer in nearby communities. Uyghurs and, indeed, the Han inhabitants were concerned about the disposal of nuclear waste in the region. PRC pressure to grow cotton was also a cause for complaint because that plant used considerable water in an area surrounded by deserts. Cotton farmers also used fertilizers and pesticides that seeped into and polluted the land and the water supply. Some non-Han also feared that the technology for extracting Xinjiang's oil and natural gas and mineral resources consumed vast amounts of water, which was siphoned away from the lands of Uyghur peasants. Moreover, they complained that the PRC and the eastern part of the country obtained Xinjiang's mineral and natural resources at little cost. The government responded that it provided considerable subsidies to Xinjiang that more than compensated for the low price of oil and natural gas.

The USSR capitalized on the chaos of the Cultural Revolution to argue that its path toward Communism was more stable than the Chinese policies and yielded the right policies. At the same time, its alleged support of Turkic identity within its own borders inspired Uyghur identity in Xinjiang, which the PRC perceived as a means of undermining its policy of greater assimilation. The new post-Mao leaders needed novel approaches in both China and Xinjiang.

NOTES

1. Ondřej Klimeš, *Struggle by the Pen: The Uyghur Discourse of National and National Interest, 1900–1949* (Leiden: Brill, 2005), 74.

2. See Rian Thum, *The Sacred Routes of Uyghur History* (Cambridge, MA: Harvard University Press, 2014).

3. David Brophy, *Uyghur Nation: Reform and Revolution on the Russia-China Frontier* (Cambridge, MA: Harvard University Press, 2016), 199.

4. Robert Tucker, *Stalin as Revolutionary, 1879–1929* (New York: Norton, 1973), 153.

5. See Justin Rudelson, *Oasis Identities: Uyghur Nationalism along China's Silk Road* (New York: Columbia University Press, 1997), 8.

6. A. Doak Barnett, *China on the Eve of Communist Takeover* (New York: Praeger, 1963), 238–60.

7. For details about the disunity among the non-Han diaspora during this time, see Justin Jacobs, *Xinjiang and the Modern Chinese State* (Seattle: University of Washington Press, 2016), 199–207.

8. Barnett, *China on the Eve of Communist Takeover*, 261.

Chapter 3

MODERATION AND ENSUING VIOLENCE, 1976–2000

ERA OF REFORM IN XINJIANG

The end of the Cultural Revolution set the stage for different policies throughout China and specifically in Xinjiang. Mao's death in 1976 led to a jockeying for power in which the radicals, who included Mao's wife, Jiang Qing, as part of the Gang of Four, were defeated within a short time. Advocates of a gradual and moderate policy took charge of the government and emphasized the economy rather than ideology. They sought economic growth through Four Modernizations—in agriculture, industry, science and technology, and defense. Economics rather than politics would inform and dictate policy. The government would condemn disruptions, mass demonstrations, and attacks on specific individuals and groups, a criticism of the damage generated during the Cultural Revolution.

The government also sought changes in Xinjiang that would lead to stability and avoid conflict among the various groups in the region. It lamented the deaths, the destruction of buildings, and the disruptive policies of the Cultural Revolution. It also recognized that it had alienated many Muslims by the razing of such religious sites as mosques, tombs, and madrassas. If it sought to stimulate economic growth in Xinjiang, it needed to curtail the withering attacks on Islam.

Even before what might be considered the official date for the end of the Cultural Revolution in 1976, the government had started to take steps to reverse course. In 1975, it abolished the *bingtuan* and reallocated its economic enterprises to local government organizations. The *bingtuan* had already been scarred because of its involvement in several of the Cultural Revolution crises. Harmed by the divisions that arose during that period, it had lost influence, and some Han within the organization had abandoned it and returned to their native regions in the central part of China. Perhaps as critical, the *bingtuan* had antagonized the Uyghurs and other non-Han by serving as a conduit for Han migration into Xinjiang.

Moderates in the central government then concluded that the non-Han ought to have greater autonomy in Xinjiang as a means of truly implementing the concept of a Xinjiang Uyghur Autonomous Region. Hu Yaobang, who would, in 1982, become general secretary of the Communist Party, visited Tibet in 1980 and bolstered that conclusion with regard not only to Tibet, but to all the minority regions. He and other leaders condemned what they termed great Han chauvinism—that is, too much control by the Han and greater pressure on the non-Han to assimilate. In the specific case of Xinjiang, they were concerned that such policies and the non-Han animosities that ensued might provide leverage for the USSR to generate more disturbances or gain greater influence in the region. They asserted that one way of combating Han chauvinism was to increase the number of non-Han cadres in the Communist Party and to rehabilitate those who had been dismissed or targeted by the Red Guards.

At the same time, greater freedom of choice as a result of the resurgence of the moderates permitted Han who had been compelled to migrate to Xinjiang to return to their native regions. Naturally, the number of Han cadres diminished somewhat. The government also offered the non-Han opportunities for better employment. Before 1976, Han settlers had had greater access to better positions in government and the economy, while most Uyghurs and other non-Han could mostly secure low-level positions. Reform meant that non-Han, especially those fluent in Chinese, could aspire to and obtain important positions. The qualifying phrase was, however, important. Knowledge of Chinese was essential for good jobs, which generated animosity from non-Chinese speakers. On the other hand, the Han argued that non-Chinese speakers could not perform the tasks required of the position.

The PRC leadership relied on economic growth as the solution to its difficulties in Xinjiang. It promoted more investment, especially linking the increasingly Han north and the predominant Uyghur south in Xinjiang. It reduced taxes and fostered cotton cultivation and extraction of natural resources, especially oil. The government and the Communist Party leaders in Xinjiang believed that a flourishing economy would, in this way, reduce tensions between Han and non-Han, and indeed some non-Han began to prosper. Yet some of these so-called reforms were self-serving and could be harmful to Xinjiang while beneficial to the state. Much of the government investment was provided to the Han, and cotton and natural resource extraction would damage Xinjiang's fragile environment while providing cheap minerals and oil to other parts of China.

The government recognized that economic growth was insufficient as a means of fostering stability. Cultural policies needed to be revamped. The government adopted a less confrontational policy concerning Islam. It rebuilt and repaired mosques, shrines, and madrassas that had been destroyed or damaged during the Cultural Revolution, although it ensured that it approved of the new leaders of these institutions. By 1990, Kashgar alone had more than one hundred mosques. The government also demanded that officials in Xinjiang not interfere with Muslim rituals, began to reprint the Koran, and permitted a select group to undertake the hajj to Mecca. In 1980, it restored the Xinjiang Islamic Association to allay concerns that it would continue the Cultural Revolution policies toward Islam. Unlike the Han, the Uyghurs and other non-Han were not subject to the one child per family restrictions initiated in 1980 to curb the rapid rate of population that strained the economy. Many non-Han were accustomed to large families, and the enforcement of such regulations on the Uyghurs and other non-Han would have elicited considerable dissatisfaction.

The PRC leadership also instructed its officials not to interfere or ban non-Han, particularly Uyghur, music and dance and publications dealing with poetry, history, and literature. There would be fewer attempts to censor Uyghur culture. In the early 1980s, a return to Arabic rather than the Latin or Cyrillic transcription for Uyghur was a decision that appealed to an even wider constituency of Uyghurs. In sum, the PRC apparently attempted to restore policies in place prior to the Great Leap Forward—policies that emphasized some autonomy, less interference in Uyghur culture, and a better economy and lifestyle, with less emphasis on ideology.

The initial phase of this policy led to some stability. Xinjiang's economy improved, and tensions between the non-Han and officials somewhat subsided. Schools and colleges returned to normal, and the government invested additional funding for education. The PRC had introduced mass, virtually universal education in Xinjiang after 1949 and replaced a rudimentary system in the madrassas based, in part, upon the Koran and other Islamic texts. In some locales in the pre-Communist period, the curriculum had consisted of boys memorizing the Koran without achieving literacy. However, secular education had arrived in some regions: "In the late 1800s, Uyghur intellectuals had been educated in Russia, Central Asia, and Turkey, and brought secular education with modern curricula to Xinjiang."[1] Nonetheless, few Uyghur students had been exposed to modern secular education until 1949. Prior to the Great Leap Forward, a modern curriculum began to be introduced, but the turbulence during the Cultural Revolution had interrupted such efforts. The architects of the new policies attempted to restore the educational system. One indication of their success was the increase in literacy rates for non-Han in Xinjiang from barely in double figures in 1949 to 75 percent by 1990.[2] That figure was still lower than in the central regions of China, but progress had been made. Xinjiang University, which the renowned China observer Doak Barnett knew as Xinjiang College and had called a "joke" during his visit in the late 1940s, had been converted into a reputable university with financial and pedagogical support from the government.

Similarly, medical care had improved after the PRC victory in 1949. Modern medicine had taken hold in Xinjiang. It was not as extensive and up-to-date as medicine in the advanced industrial countries. Yet the government established clinics and hospitals and trained so-called barefoot doctors who could provide rudimentary care for those in remote areas of the region. The Great Leap Forward and the Cultural Revolution had disrupted this system, and the moderates now sought to restore this kind of care and to create greater stability in health care. By 1998, the policy appeared to be successful. Xinjiang had 2.7 doctors per 1,000 people in its cities and 1.7 in its counties, while the national average was 2.6 and 1.1, respectively.[3]

The government and many Han could not understand Uyghur grievances in light of the health, educational, and welfare benefits accruing to Xinjiang and its non-Han population as a result of PRC policies. Food was plentiful as compared to pre-1949 times, and labor-saving devices, such as washing machines, began to be more widespread. The government also asserted that *begs*, or a small elite, had exploited the vast majority of the non-Han population in the pre-1949 period; and poverty, food insecurity, a short life span, and poor access to modern medicine and education had prevailed. Yet it did not initially acknowledge that the Uyghurs had fewer employment prospects and lower wages than Han workers.

Whatever the attitudes of the Han and non-Han, conditions in Xinjiang in the late 1970s and early 1980s improved, but problems persisted. The return to private plots of land and elimination of communes led to an increase in agricultural production. Yet the household registration system, which replaced the communes and was the basis for taxation, still imposed obligations on peasants, both Han and non-Han. The government received part of the crops and could mandate that peasants grow specific goods, such as cotton. State industries were started but were not as successful due to inefficiencies and, in some cases, insufficient investment. They were also plagued by accidents because of inadequate safety standards. To be sure, investment increased, but the government still favored economic growth in the eastern and coastal parts of China more than in the interior, including Xinjiang, which did not witness the same economic vitality.

In 1982, the government, disappointed by the lags in economic growth in Xinjiang, made the fateful decision of restoring the *bingtuan*, which engendered Uyghur suspicion and then enmity. Within a few years, the *bingtuan*'s factories and farms contributed one quarter of Xinjiang's total production. It also governed at least five towns and built its own hospitals, schools, and recreational centers. The government had planned to have the *bingtuan* support the new economic policies, as well as the new attitudes toward the non-Han, which stressed greater autonomy.

More controversial was that the *bingtuan*, of which almost 90 percent consisted of Han, provided assistance and employment for Han migrants and thus served as a mechanism for greater immigration to Xinjiang, a central issue of concern for non-Han.

On the other hand, although the government compelled or urged Han to move to Xinjiang, many had left in the early stages of reform in the late 1970s. The government's policy was inconsistent because, by the early 1980s, other Han had been forced to stay and resented their inability to return to their families in the central part of China. Frustration led to unpleasant incidents with the non-Han. As early as 1980, in a well-publicized event a couple of Han beat up a Uyghur in the town of Aksu. In the non-Han majority areas south of the Tianshan Mountains, including the cities of Yarkand and Kashgar, the Han were, on occasion, the victims of attacks.

One change was the improvement in China's and therefore Xinjiang's relations with the USSR. In the late 1970s, the Sino-Soviet border was tense. Non-Han in Xinjiang often had more in common with the Turkic and Muslim peoples on the Soviet side of the border than with the Han, which could pose a potential problem for China. At the same time, Soviet troops moved into Afghanistan in 1979, leading to a struggle with the Islamic fundamentalists known as the mujahideen. The Chinese leaders were distressed that the USSR's involvement in Afghanistan enabled the Soviets to be ominously close to Xinjiang and could potentially block the routes from China to Pakistan, a Chinese ally. Soviet criticism of China in its conflict with Vietnam in 1979 added to the Chinese leaders' concerns. Tension resulted in minor clashes along the border, compelling China to station more troops on the frontiers and to place guards around Xinjiang's capital, Urumchi, and its nuclear testing site in Lop Nor, also in Xinjiang. Meanwhile the Soviets also had numerous troops stationed along the border and may have had as many as 100,000 soldiers along the Chinese border in Mongolia. By the early 1980s, military expenditures for both sides were increasing in an unsustainable way. The financial burdens finally compelled an easing of tensions in the early 1980s, with the preliminary step of cross-border commerce. The Central Asian regions of the USSR and Xinjiang began to engage in trade, an effective means of dissipating conflicts. Shortly thereafter, border incidents between the two countries' military forces decreased. Both developments contributed to somewhat greater stability and economic gains in Xinjiang.

Hu Yaobang, the general secretary of the Communist Party and an avid reformer, visited Xinjiang in 1983 and called for policies to promote stability. He emphasized that non-Han should be granted greater autonomy and that more of them should be recruited as Communist Party cadres. Such moderation culminated in the Law on Regional Autonomy for Minority Nationalities of 1984, which, in theory, offered several concessions to the minorities in China. The law gave some authority to the regional people's congresses and mandated representation for the minorities in that and other government bodies. The top position in the regional government would often be reserved for a minority member, thus allowing minorities some leverage on such issues as health care, the environment, and culture. Nonetheless, the central government would dominate the military, the courts, public security, and the Communist Party, the real loci of power in the region. The People's Liberation Army had complete jurisdiction over local forces; the supreme court could override local courts, undermining their judicial authority; and the central government's State Council limited the authority of the regional legislatures.

Yet distance from the capital city of Beijing and the government's primary attention to other areas translated into somewhat greater flexibility for local officials in Xinjiang. Transport and communications from Beijing to Xinjiang were still cumbersome through the early to mid-1980s, which placed limits on the central government's inspection and domination. Moreover, the central government was focusing on economic development along the east coast, which, as a consequence, meant that it paid less attention to such inland and more remote areas as Xinjiang. Because there were also no major disturbances among the non-Han in Xinjiang, the central government leaders did not need to devote as much time and effort to the region. This lack of attention was a two-edged sword. On the one hand, it meant less central government intrusion in Xinjiang, but on the other hand, it translated into slower economic growth than in the east coast provinces. Such unequal economic development would eventually generate grievances among the non-Han in Xinjiang.

By 1985, stability had returned to Xinjiang, which was a decided relief for the population that had lived through the unsettled and chaotic Cultural Revolution. The government prized economic progress more than Communist ideology. Pragmatism and policies that promoted economic growth superseded adherence to strict doctrines. Until 1989, only minor incidents marred the relatively placid circumstances. To be sure, the new policies faced impediments. For example, some Han officials did not carry out the moderate policies the government espoused, alienating, in particular, Uyghur intellectuals and writers who since the late 1970s had capitalized on greater state flexibility to write essays, historical novels, and poetry emphasizing Uyghur identity. A few officials sought to limit such publications. At the same time, some Han technical specialists needed for economic development in Xinjiang wished to return to their homelands in the central regions of China, which was an impediment to economic growth in Xinjiang. It would also undermine efforts to implement the government policy of encouraging non-Han assimilation and intermarriage with the Han. The government did not reassign these Han specialists to their native regions and compelled them to remain in Xinjiang as part of a policy to promote Han migration into Xinjiang, antagonizing both the Han and the non-Han.

The non-Han also took part in incidents in opposition to government policies. In 1985, Uyghur students at the Central Nationalities Institute in Beijing protested the use of Lop Nor, in Xinjiang, as a nuclear testing site. They noted, in particular, the increased rate of cancer in neighboring areas. The demonstration was tame, and the students dispersed without violence. Yet the government did not promise to end the nuclear tests. Uyghurs complained that there were numerous Han cadres and only a relatively few non-Han cadres; and the *bingtuan*, composed of Han, still played an outsized role in the Xinjiang economy. Other non-Han complaints concerned the government's demand that farmers plant cotton, which consumed considerable amounts of water and entailed the use of pesticides and fertilizers that damaged the land and depleted the water resources. Local inhabitants also resented the state's emphasis on natural resource extraction rather than developing manufacturing in Xinjiang. Uyghur farmers were concerned that water for agriculture would be diminished because of its use in mining and drilling. Moreover, they protested that the discovery of oil in new locations in Xinjiang resulted in the arrival of additional Han workers. Yet violence did not erupt.

UYGHUR PROTESTS START IN 1990

The relative calm after the Cultural Revolution began to unravel in 1989, the same year as the Tiananmen incident during which the PRC clamped down on students and others in Beijing's main square. Peace in both the central part of the country and in Xinjiang had concealed dissatisfaction. The funeral in April of

1989 of Hu Yaobang, the moderate leader, had prompted tens of thousands to organize a march to Tiananmen, the principal square in Beijing, to protest his earlier dismissal from office in 1987. This demonstration would evolve into an occupation of the square in Tiananmen for a month and a half until the army and police cracked down on June 4. Government forces killed quite a number of protestors and observers in clearing the square. Hu's death had also reverberated in Xinjiang because he had been the principal supporter and architect of the new policies for Uyghurs and other non-Han. An indication of the dissatisfaction of some Uyghurs was that one of the leaders of the Tiananmen square students was the Uyghur Wu'erkaixi (1968–), a student at Beijing Normal University who eventually migrated to Taiwan.

In Xinjiang itself, the non-Han had complaints despite the policy of reform since the Cultural Revolution. They noted that they had lower wages than the Han and had only limited access to high-level jobs because of a "glass ceiling." They protested that some of the *bingtuan* controlled the most skilled and highest paying jobs in energy and mineral and natural resource extraction. Their rate of unemployment was also higher than those of the Han. Han employers countered that many positions required knowledge of the Chinese language, which ruled out many Uyghurs. Employers argued that they did not discriminate and that the non-Han often did not possess the education for employment that required advanced skills. The government asserted that its policy of affirmative action in education and employment was designed to remedy such difficulties. Finally, the government argued that it had invested considerable sums in energy and infrastructure projects in Xinjiang in order to bolster employment. Yet some Uyghurs and other non-Han did not find these arguments persuasive. They asserted that discrimination, pure and simple, prevented their economic advancement. As in the past, they were concerned about the continuing Han migration and the expanding role of Han in the economy and the system of justice.

Social and religious, not economic or educational, issues actually led to violence. Although the government had devised a one child per family policy in 1980, it had not been applied to the Uyghurs and other minorities. By the late 1980s, however, the central authorities sought to limit the so-called national minorities to two or three children, which the Uyghurs considered to be a threat to their survival. At the same time, the government began to perceive Islam as a subversive force promoting what it called "splittism," or separation from China to organize an independent state. The establishment of mosques or meeting places that did not register with the government concerned the state and Communist Party authorities in Xinjiang. They considered secret institutions as threats and condemned and tried to root them out. The growth of fundamentalist and Muslim movements around the world strengthened the government's resolve to suppress so-called Islamic separatists and, at the same time, offered justification for such crackdowns.

A violent incident finally erupted in April of 1990. The circumstances concerning this incident are murky, and there are different versions of the events. One provided by the PRC is that a demonstration in Baren, a town near Kashgar, led by militants opposed to the regulations about supervision of mosques, prompted the government to send two Chinese cadres to negotiate a peaceful resolution. Instead, the demonstrators murdered the two, catching the government by surprise. It had not anticipated violence and had assumed that the demonstrators would not harm the two envoys. Even after the killings, the government seemed unaware of the scale of the uprising. It sent a detachment of police and public security officials to control the demonstrators, but the authorities found themselves in a pitched battle, as the demonstrators possessed weapons, some of which were smuggled in from Afghanistan or Central Asia. A larger unit of the People's Liberation Army was required to overwhelm the Uyghur and Kyrgyz uprising. The number of casualties is in dispute, with the government claiming that only a small group was killed.[4]

Two other versions offer differing views of the violence. One that originated from the Uyghur expatriates is that several hundred demonstrators surrounded a government building in a peaceful protest against religious discrimination and oppressive government and Communist Party policies. Army forces attacked the demonstrators and killed hundreds. Another version that appears again to have originated from government sources is that an organization called the Eastern Turkistan Islamic Party, which objected to PRC religious policies and was particularly concerned about restrictions on the number of births and on forced abortions for non-Han, planned an uprising, in hopes that the inhabitants of the nearby city of Kashgar would join. On April 5, the group acted, surrounding the offices of the local government and killing several policemen sent to assist the beleaguered officials. Violence erupted, and the authorities needed to call on army units, with helicopters and artillery, to overwhelm the dissidents.[5] The group had explosives but little other firepower. Yet, some arms were probably smuggled in from nearby countries. The Chinese army killed the leader and at least sixteen of his men and executed at least three others, but the authorities in Xinjiang provided few other details about others who were arrested. All that is known is that government forces quickly crushed the rebels.

GOVERNMENT RESPONSES TO PROTESTS

The government drew lessons from this event that would shape its policies throughout the 1990s. First, it recognized that Islam could be a unifying force for non-Han in Xinjiang. The government asserted that mosques, madrassas, and shrines had to be carefully regulated. If they espoused what the government would call separatism, then they would be suppressed. To be sure, officials recognized that prominent shrines and mosques could be turned into tourist sites for Muslims from abroad and for non-Han travelers from other regions in Xinjiang, but the government viewed these institutions as potential threats. It was also concerned that some Muslim groups in Central Asia who were agitating for change and would soon form independent states, as the USSR broke up, could be a source of support for Uyghurs and other non-Han. After all, some of the weapons available to the demonstrators in Baren appear to have originated from neighboring Central Asian regions. The government faced a dilemma. It sought to limit contacts between the Central Asian regions and Xinjiang, particularly with the Uyghurs and Kazakhs from Xinjiang who had fled to Central Asia prior to and during the Cultural Revolution. At the same time, it wanted to foster Xinjiang's trade with Central Asia and was eager to obtain natural gas from Turkmenistan and oil from Kazakhstan. The collapse of the USSR and the creation of separate Central Asian countries, which had Muslim majorities in their populations, exacerbated China's concerns in the early 1990s.

The government's analysis of the Baren incident led to a return to a less flexible policy toward expressions of ethnic identity. It imposed strict censorship on Uyghur books and music and weeded out any indication in histories and songs that smacked of what it would consider as separatism, or what others might conceive of as an assertion of ethnic pride. On a minor note, it also overrode any objections of the use of Beijing time for all parts of the country, including Xinjiang, without consideration of time zones, which the Uyghur population found to be irritating. Uyghurs and other non-Han continued to use their own time, but Beijing time remained official and a tangible indication of the central government's maintaining control.

Yet the most significant policies focused on Islam. Xinjiang's leaders in government asserted that they were concerned about fundamentalist Muslims, but their regulations affected other Muslims as well. They closed down many small mosques, which had not registered with the state. They ensured that mosque leaders received their training in the Institute for the Study of Islamic Texts in Urumchi under government and Communist Party supervision because the state had to ensure that they were reliable before approving them for their positions. Officials sent agents to observe ceremonies and prayers at mosques. They also instructed Communist Party members not to fast during Ramadan, to abjure Islam, to avoid exposure to the Koran, and to adopt atheism. Schools were given the responsibility of diminishing the role of religion, and therefore children under the age of eighteen could attend neither services at mosques nor meetings in study groups.

The government determined that economic development was essential to defuse tensions in Xinjiang and to prevent another Baren crisis. Since 1978, economic growth had centered upon China's east coast, which left Xinjiang behind and had contributed to non-Han dissatisfaction. Under a new policy that emphasized economic growth in Xinjiang, the *bingtuan* would play a major role in such economic plans as development of the infrastructure of roads and railroads, irrigation for cotton production on state farms, and petrochemical industries, the latter of which also entailed the import of gas and oil from Central Asia. These economic tasks would have the effect of encouraging more Han migrants to work in these projects; and by 1992, the *bingtuan* consisted of more than two million, mostly Han workers. In theory, however, the Uyghurs and other non-Han would also benefit from economic growth.

These policies provoked criticism. Some Uyghurs feared Han migration, which could eventually lead to the non-Han becoming a minority in the region, and they still remained concerned that the Han secured the best employment. Although intermarriage between the Han and the Uyghurs had been limited, the large-scale arrival of Han could presage such unions. As noted earlier, the Uyghur critics noted that cotton cultivation posed environmental threats to lands in Xinjiang with scarce water supplies. Introduction of more agriculture and use of water for irrigation, as well as oil exploration and production, could damage and degrade pastureland and perhaps lead to deforestation in the Yili region of northern Xinjiang. They also argued that emphasis on oil production and extraction of mineral resources without concomitant investment in industry could lead Xinjiang to depend on the central regions in China for manufactured goods.

Even the government's seemingly benevolent affirmative action policies for the non-Han generated hostility from some Han and non-Han. In Xinjiang, the required score in the liberal arts college entrance exams for admission to the best universities for the Han was 415, while the score for non-Han admission was 330. In the sciences, the Han required a score for 415; the score for non-Han was 315.[6] Many Han resented such policies because they believed that they would be at a disadvantage in education and employment. Even some Uyghurs opposed the policies because the successes they would have in schools and work would be attributed to the favoritism associated with the affirmative action policies.

These problems notwithstanding, the latter half of the 1990s witnessed economic gains and prosperity in Xinjiang. Oil, agriculture, construction of infrastructure, and larger populations in urban areas offered attractive opportunities for employment and careers. For the first time since 1949, the government did not have to compel Han settlers to move into Xinjiang. They arrived voluntarily, and most settled in northern Xinjiang, as the south remained primarily a Uyghur or non-Han zone. Han migrants who had been on the fringes of society in eastern China became aware of the prospects for employment in Xinjiang. Peasants received favorable leases on land, as well as tax abatements. They did not need to worry about losing their household registrations (*hukou*) in their native provinces because the government actively encouraged resettlement in Xinjiang. In 1999, Jiang Zemin, the general secretary of the Communist Party and the president of the PRC, contributed to this in-migration when he announced a program for developing the west (*yibu dakaifa*), which included Xinjiang and neighboring provinces. The rate of poverty for the Uyghurs also declined, although they did not make the same gains as the Han.

Even as early as 1998, Xinjiang was among the top ten recipients of capital investment in China's provinces or autonomous regions. Moreover, "Xinjiang, in terms of the national rankings for per capita investment and per capita investment for the entire period from 1953 to 1998, had the best results among the northwestern provinces and autonomous regions."[7] Local expenditures were higher than local revenues, so the PRC was subsidizing Xinjiang. Yet, there was a disparity in incomes in Han and non-Han regions. Most of the largest enterprises, many of which managed extractive industries, were in Han areas in northern Xinjiang, and the managers of large and medium-sized enterprises were Han. Yet again, the authorities claimed that the non-Han had not as yet developed the skills necessary for such positions. They asserted that the south, which housed a majority of the Uyghurs, required additional assistance because it was less industrialized and poorer and had a higher fertility rate. More investment in basics, such as education and development of skills, was needed. Despite the disparities in income between Han and non-Han, the economy of Xinjiang improved.

However, economic growth did not translate into less violence. Some Uyghurs appeared to be better off, but a significant minority was dissatisfied and alienated. The continual Han in-migration, the differential in incomes and employment opportunities between Han and non-Han, the economic and political power of the *bingtuan*, the restrictions on the practice of Islam, the limitations on the expressions of Uyghur culture and language, the advantages accruing to excellent facility in the Chinese language in employment, and the mutual stereotypes of Han and Uyghurs grated on the sensitivities of some Uyghurs. Several protested that the PRC gained access to Xinjiang's mineral and natural resources at a lower cost relative to prices on the world market. The government responded that it provided manufactured goods to Xinjiang at a similarly low cost and that it had also made substantial investments in the region's infrastructure. Moreover, it noted that Xinjiang received considerable subsidies from the state. This response did not win over the Uyghur critics. Still another cause of tension was the nuclear testing in Xinjiang. In 1998, Dr. Enver Tohti, a surgeon who had secretly examined official documents that confirmed a high incidence of cancer, perhaps as much as 35 percent higher than expected, around the test areas, was the adviser on a British documentary that depicted the threat that nuclear testing posed. Shortly thereafter, he departed and sought asylum in Great Britain after having publicized the Communist policy and propaganda, which downplayed the dangers of nuclear testing.

Several non-Han groups sought independence from China, but most simply wanted greater autonomy. The PRC government was concerned about those demanding independence, partly in light of developments right across the border. PRC leaders believed that the collapse of the USSR in the early 1990s and the establishment of independent Central Asian states had created vulnerabilities in Xinjiang. The breakup of the Soviet Union particularly worried the leaders, who believed that the USSR's weakness and its debates about and challenges to Communist ideology had precipitated its downfall and led the various minorities in Central Asia to establish their own governments. The PRC was worried that the new political situation in Central Asia could serve as a model for those Uyghurs and non-Han seeking their own state, or what the government considered to be "splittism." Could events across the border in Russia inspire non-Han in Xinjiang to demand their own state? PRC leaders also feared that Islamic fundamentalists in Central Asia, Afghanistan, and Pakistan, all areas just west of Xinjiang, would influence the non-Han to adopt a militant posture. These neighboring states could, in theory, serve as havens for radical Uyghurs and foster in them fundamentalist ideologies and could provide practical military training.

The PRC was certainly concerned about the role of Central Asia in promoting ethnic separatism, but it also coveted oil from Kazakhstan and Uzbekistan and natural gas from Turkmenistan. It first needed to reduce tensions with these new Central Asian countries, and it had started, in 1992, by establishing formal diplomatic relations with each of them. Trade with Kazakhstan, which shared a common border with China and boasted good roads and fine transport facilities, was particularly significant. The next step was resolution of delineation of the borders with Kazakhstan, Kyrgystan, and Tajikistan, which was accomplished by 1999. Chinese leaders also sought cross-border cooperation on arms smuggling, which worried them because dissidents and fundamentalists could potentially gain access to lethal weapons. Another major concern was the Uyghurs and other non-Han who had fled to Central Asia from 1949 on, started activist movements demanding Xinjiang independence, and were in touch with fundamentalists within Xinjiang.

The PRC was determined to demand that the five Central Asian countries restrict the activities of the activists and employ economic leverage to influence the Central Asian governments. A flurry of economic activity had resulted in a doubling of trade between China and Central Asia from 1992 to 1997. The Central Asian states, aware of the importance of commerce with China, began to alter some of their policies to avoid alienating China. By the mid-1990s, they started to impose controls on the Uyghurs and other Turkic people within their borders. They curbed the Uyghurs' propaganda, which proposed autonomy. The president of Kazakhstan said, "If China stands against separatist movements, we in Kazakhstan will also stand against . . . separatist movements."[8]

Kazakhstan and Kyrgyzstan banned Uyghurs from organizing pedagogical and military training sessions, and in 1996, the Central Asian states signed agreements with China to prevent Uyghur "terrorists." Islam Karimov himself, the ruler of Uzbekistan, faced a radical Muslim group, known as the Islamic Movement of Uzbekistan, and supported a repressive policy toward fundamentalists. The culmination of these steps occurred in 1996 when Russia and China convened a meeting with four of the five Central Asian states, exclusive of Uzbekistan. The two great powers secured Central Asian cooperation in curbing ethnic and religious dissenters, which, for China, translated into control of the Uyghurs in Central Asia. From that time on, the Central Asian countries clamped down on Uyghurs living within their borders who advocated independence for Xinjiang.[9]

INCREASES IN VIOLENCE AND "STRIKE HARD"

The 1990 Baren incident was not the only evidence of violence. In 1992, Uyghur radicals triggered a bomb in two buses in Urumchi, leaving six people dead and twenty or so injured. They also detonated bombs in Khotan, Kashgar, Yining, and other cities. PRC leaders blamed these deadly attacks on the machinations of Uyghurs living abroad. The establishment of a Uyghur Liberation Organization in Kazakhstan prompted the Chinese leadership to be concerned about developments there. The authorities in the PRC, therefore, sought collaboration with the Central Asian countries or pressured their governments to impose limits on Uyghurs in their lands. The assassination of the Chinese ambassador to Kyrgyzstan, which was blamed on Uyghurs, exacerbated PRC concerns.

Despite the acquiescence of the Central Asian countries, violence continued to erupt. In July of 1995 in Khotan, a demonstration objecting to the government's removal of two religious leaders from their positions led to a confrontation with the police. Estimates of casualties are difficult to verify. One of the most publicized incidents was the attempted assassination, in May of 1996, of the imam of the most prominent mosque in Kashgar. One source has enumerated nineteen bombings, assassinations and failed assassination attempts, and robberies and murders from 1990 to 1999.[10]

In February of 1997, a serious incident involving Uyghurs broke out in Yining, an unusual venue for such difficulties. Yining was in the north, where Kazakhs constituted the majority, although Han and Uyghurs had also settled in the region. Once again, religion played a role. The local government had raided a study meeting (*mäshräp*) at a mosque that had not received a government license and authorization, and arrested a few students.

Demonstrators demanded the release of the students, and then fighting broke out, during which demonstrators attacked police officers and Han inhabitants, and the police, abetted by army forces, killed some of the demonstrators.

The government quickly imposed a curfew and initiated house-to-house searches, which led to the arrest, imprisonment, and alleged torture of so-called perpetrators of the violence. Each side blamed the other for the outbreak. More important, the Yining incident was followed by the Uyghur detonation of bombs on public buses in Urumchi, which led to the deaths of nine people, and in Beijing within the same month. The authorities captured so-called splittists and executed several of those involved. Over the next few years, the government reported a larger number of executions, and numerous Uyghurs were arrested. Reports about the torture of prisoners circulated throughout Xinjiang, though they could not be verified.

PRC leaders attributed this "splittist" violence to Muslim fundamentalists, often based in mosques and in discussion groups. It asserted that much of the radical ideology derived from Central Asia, Afghanistan, and, increasingly, Pakistan. The PRC determined that the more moderate and tolerant government policies that had prevailed since 1979 needed to be reversed, and ideologies imported from abroad had to be circumscribed or eliminated. Students and others who went to Afghanistan and Pakistan and attended madrassas in Pakistan had to be more carefully monitored. Otherwise, they would return to China with radical Islamic views. In general, a tougher policy was required to end the disturbances.

"Strike Hard" would be the slogan for this new policy. The government initiated this approach slightly before the violence in Yining. The Strike Hard campaign defined nearly all opponents who sought independence for Xinjiang as "splittists." There was no fine-tuning, which might have defined opponents as seekers of greater autonomy or more freedom of expression in arts and culture. Even protectors of the Uyghur environment, which was afflicted with nuclear testing, desertification, mining debris, and misuse of limited water supplies for irrigation of cotton, were stigmatized. The PRC leadership often did not distinguish among these various groups and referred to nearly all of them as "splittists."

Strike Hard also focused on the Uyghur diaspora in Central Asia and other locations who called for independence as well as on religious leaders engaged in "illegal activities." Government regulations directed officials to pay more attention to the threats that radical Islamic leaders posed. Such a strong stance necessitated restraints on Islam, including prevention of publication of "subversive works" and limitations on the exposure of young people to religious teachings. Shortly thereafter, a campaign began to place additional restrictions on religion. Officials suspended or banned the building of new mosques, monitored the training and political education of imams, and kept a close watch on madrassas. They also engaged in more aggressive actions, as befitted the slogan "Strike Hard." Police and army forces undertook house-to-house searches and rounded up thousands of so-called separatists who were tried and then jailed. Some of the prisoners were indeed Uyghurs who sought independence or greater autonomy, but some others were simply accused of "illegal religious activities." Avid religious expression was stigmatized and perceived to represent separatism.

Religious influences from Afghanistan, where the fundamentalist Taliban had taken charge in 1996, and Pakistan, where Uyghur fundamentalists were training, had to be excluded as well. Trade with Pakistan over the newly constructed Karakoram highway, would persist, but the PRC instructed its officials to be vigilant about Uyghur merchants and students traveling there. As part of the Strike Hard campaign, radical Islam had to be extirpated in Xinjiang. In any event, bombings still bedeviled the PRC leadership throughout 1998 and 1999, but Strike Hard emboldened the government to employ harsh measures.

Perhaps Strike Hard's most prominent target was Rebiya Kadeer, a Uyghur businesswoman who became a multimillionaire. Even during the height of the Cultural Revolution, she had developed her entrepreneurial skills by making and selling clothing, which the Chinese authorities labeled a "secret business" and for which they castigated her for her bourgeois activities. She asserted that the local leaders retaliated by pressuring her husband of twelve years to divorce her. Despite such opposition, she still capitalized on the liberalization of the economy, after Mao's death in 1976, to operate a laundry, from there to ownership of a department store, and finally involvement in cross-border trade with Russia and Central Asia. By the early 1990s, she had become the richest woman in China and served as a delegate to the Chinese People's Consultative Conference. As a celebrity, she met Bill Gates and Warren Buffett during their tour of China. Her wealth also permitted her to fund a 1,000 Mothers' Movement that assisted Uyghur women in starting their own businesses and in helping institutions in caring for orphans, which were both noteworthy contributions.

Her life changed dramatically when her second husband, Sidiq Rouzi, a professor and Uyghur nationalist, emigrated to the United States in 1996 and became a broadcaster for Radio Free Asia and the Voice of America and a frequent critic of the PRC's policies toward Uyghurs. Through her sources in government, she obtained secret documents about Uyghur demonstrations and PRC fears about Xinjiang, which she then transmitted to her husband. Learning of her involvement in dispatching these smuggled documents to her husband, the authorities arrested her in August of 1999. In March of 2000, she was tried and found guilty of leaking state secrets and of contacting separatist leaders. She was imprisoned, but intense international pressure finally led to her release on medical grounds in 2005, and she moved to the Washington, DC, area. Elected president of the World Uyghur Congress in 2006 and remaining in that office until 2017, she has been an ardent advocate of Uyghur independence and a thorn in the side of the PRC, which has blamed her for inciting violence.

The World Uyghur Congress, based in Munich and founded in 2004, is one of a number of diaspora organizations that emphasize human rights, PRC oppression in Xinjiang, and preservation of Uyghur culture. The Uyghur American Congress, which was established in 1998, had the same objectives. Both organizations receive grants from the National Endowment for Democracy, which, in turn, receives its funding from the US Congress. This support has allowed the PRC to portray them as agents of the US government and to accuse Rebiya Kadeer of instigating unrest in Xinjiang.

Despite her seemingly benevolent actions, Rebiya Kadeer published an autobiography titled *Dragon Fighter: One Woman's Epic Struggle for Peace with China*, which further antagonized the PRC.[11] Her message was "liberate the Uyghur nation from its occupiers," and she described her entrepreneurial success as a mission, asserting, "God, I've undertaken this business in your name." Such comments and her relationships with US officials, including President George W. Bush and congressmen and congresswomen, offered publicity for the Uyghur cause. However, her demands for complete independence for the Uyghurs did not sit well with the PRC.

NOTES

1. Yangbin Chen, *Muslim Uyghur Students in a Chinese Boarding School* (Lanham, MD: Lexington, 2008), 35.

2. A. S. Bhalla and Shufang Qiu, *Poverty and Inequality among Chinese Minorities* (New York: Routledge, 2006), 77. The literacy rate among the Han was 87 percent.

3. Bhalla and Qiu, *Poverty and Inequality among Chinese Minorities*, 106.

4. Nick Holdstock, *China's Forgotten People: Xinjiang, Terror, and the Chinese State* (London: Tauris, 2015), 49–50.

5. James Millward, *Eurasian Crossroads: A History of Xinjiang* (New York: Columbia University Press, 2007), 325–27.

6. Rongxing Guo, *China's Spatial (Dis)integration: Political Economy of the Interethnic Unrest in Xinjiang* (Waltham, MA: Chandos Publishing, 2015), 131.

7. David Bachman, "Making Xinjiang Safe for the Han" in Morris Rossabi, ed., *Governing China's Multiethnic Frontiers* (Seattle: University of Washington Press, 2004), 165.

8. Sean Roberts, "A Land of 'Borderlands': Implications of Xinjiang's Trans-border Interactions," in Frederick S. Starr, ed., *Xinjiang: China's Muslim Borderland* (Armonk, NY: Sharpe, 2004), 233.

9. For additional details, see Morris Rossabi, "China and Central Asia: Developing Relations and Impact on Democracy," in Shiping Hua, ed., *Islam and Democratization in Asia* (Amherst, NY: Cambria Press, 2009), 287–310.

10. J. Todd Reed and Diana Rashchke, *The ETIM: China's Militants and the Global Terrorist Threat* (Santa Barbara, CA: Greenwood, 2010), 55–62.

11. Rebiya Kadeer, *Dragon Fighter: One Woman's Struggle for Peace with China* (Carlsbad, CA: Kales Press, 2011).

4

"CARROTS AND STICKS" IN THE TWENTY-FIRST CENTURY

At the end of the twentieth century, the PRC leadership began to develop a "carrots and sticks" approach to Xinjiang. On the one hand, China promoted strong state support for economic growth, as well as specific benefits such as affirmative action for the Uyghurs. This strategy would appeal to moderate Uyghurs and might also tone down the concerns of Muslim countries, which might accuse China of anti-Islamic policies. On the other hand, the "Strike Hard" campaign emphasized repression of so-called terrorists, extremists, and separatists. Large contingents of police and army would be stationed throughout the region, and the army would be present in the public venues in the predominantly non-Han areas. The government would impose harsh penalties, with the liberal use of executions. It labeled terrorism, separatism, and religious extremism as the "three evils."

SHANGHAI COOPERATION ORGANIZATION, 9/11 AFTEREFFECTS VERSUS MODERATION

Nonetheless, violence persisted in Xinjiang and Central Asia, prompting the establishment of a more formal regional organization to combat the threat of "radical Islam." In June of 2001,

Russia and China gathered together representatives from Kazakhstan, Kyrgyzstan, and Tajikistan to create the Shanghai Cooperation Organization (SCO). Uzbekistan, which had refrained from earlier collaborations, now joined the SCO after an assassination attempt on the head of state, Islam Karimov. Of the Central Asian states, only Turkmenistan and its head of state, Saparmyrat Niyazov, who proclaimed himself "Turkmenbashi," or Father of the Turkmen, did not send representatives to the meeting. The SCO mandate emphasized security against terrorism, but the PRC had another objective in mind as well. It sought to use the SCO as a means of reducing the threat that the Uyghurs and other non-Han dissenters in Central Asia represented.

China and Russia also appear to have perceived of the SCO as an antidote to the North Atlantic Treaty Organization (NATO). As NATO had expanded its membership to include Russia's Eastern European neighbors, Russia and China sought to attract the support of their Asian neighbors. With that kind of leverage, China could have greater influence over Central Asian policy concerning ethnic and religious resurgence. The PRC gained support due, in part, to economic developments. Trade turnover between China and Central Asia increased from about $1.8 billion in 2000 to approximately $7.7 billion in 2005. Energy would replace consumer goods as the main item in commerce. Transport of energy resources required the PRC to build pipelines, railroads, and roads throughout the region. Economic influence and deals with the states in the region led to greater cooperation with China on the Uyghurs living both within Xinjiang and Central Asia. No one could foresee that just three months after the founding of the SCO, one event could dramatically transform policy and attitudes toward Central Asia and Xinjiang.

The transformative events of the al-Qaeda movement's airplane attacks on New York City and Washington, DC, along with the crash of one plane in Pennsylvania, on September 11, 2001, had a profound impact on the PRC's relations with Central Asia and on its policies in Xinjiang. This catastrophe unleashed on the World Trade Center in New York City and on the Pentagon in the Washington, DC, area by a few radical Muslims in al-Qaeda reverberated around the world and contributed to anti-Muslim perceptions in countries where Islam was in the minority. Indeed, Xinjiang's Muslims, together with the Hui or ethnic Chinese Muslims found throughout the country, were a tiny minority in the PRC, whose mostly Han leaders were bolstered by the 9/11 terrorists in their views of the threat that Islamic separatists posed. They quickly condemned the attack and ramped up the campaign against "terrorism, separatism, and religious extremism."

Officials asserted that Xinjiang's separatists had links to the international terrorist movement, as represented by al-Qaeda. Based on that supposition, they claimed that the indigenous separatists belonged to one terrorist organization, the East Turkistan Islamic Movement or ETIM, which was founded in 1997 and was allegedly responsible for most of the violence. A study by J. Todd Reed and Diana Raschke of the violent incidents does not support the claim of a single organization masterminding these events. In fact, Reed and Raschke listed twenty-six separate militant organizations in Xinjiang, although a number of them were small operations.[1] Many of these organizations developed because of local grievances, and a link to a single group, such as ETIM, cannot be attested. The PRC accused several of them, including the ETIM, of raising funds through robberies and involvement in drug traffic and arms smuggling. It is impossible to verify this charge. In any case, almost a year after 9/11, the US State Department corroborated the PRC contention and placed the ETIM on the list of terrorist organizations and associated it with al-Qaeda. Reed and Raschke concurred: "The ETIM is a terrorist organization that demands an independent fundamentalist state for the Uyghur ethnic minority in northwest China."[2] Its leaders conceived of the restoration of the Islamic caliphate, and some would collaborate with and seek assistance from al-Qaeda and the Taliban.

The United States might have labeled it a terrorist organization to avoid Chinese criticism of efforts to establish American military bases in Uzbekistan and Kyrgyzstan in its campaign against al-Qaeda in Afghanistan. Another motivation may have been to ingratiate itself with the PRC in return for acquiescence to a United States' invasion of Iraq. Whatever the explanation, the PRC began to portray any dissent or violence as linked to the ETIM. The US engagement in Afghanistan yielded even more support for the PRC's position. US forces captured twenty-two Uyghurs who had trained with the fundamentalist Taliban and may have been planning to cross into Xinjiang to create unrest.

The concept of ETIM provided justification for additional restrictions and regulations. Within a few months after 9/11, the PRC increased the number of crimes for which capital punishment was mandated, a new policy aimed especially at separatists or religious extremists. Strike Hard persisted, and some critics accused the PRC of setting up quotas for arrests in each region, compelling local officials to imprison innocent people, an assertion that cannot be verified. The government also demanded enforcement of the laws concerning Islam; imams could hold services only at mosques, not in private locations, and Muslims under eighteen years of age could not attend a mosque.

As on most occasions except for the Cultural Revolution, a moderate policy accompanied the more demanding regulations. This moderate approach entailed education. Uyghur schools, in which Uyghur was the official language, were not regarded as highly as the Chinese schools, and *minkaomin*, the Uyghur students in these schools, were not as proficient in Chinese. Because most high-level employment required fluency in Chinese, the *minkaomin* were at a disadvantage in the competition for jobs. In response, the Chinese government registered some Uyghur students, known as *minkaohan*, in the mostly Chinese schools. Reports about the *minkaohan* differ. The anthropologist Joanne Smith Finley presented a mixed portrait of the *minkaohan*: they were neither entirely Han nor Uyghur; they often spoke better Chinese than Uyghur but were not necessarily accepted as part of Han society; some became divorced from Uyghur culture whereas others, as parents, wanted their children to learn the Uyghur language before Chinese; many were aware of Han feelings of superiority, whereas others perceived themselves to have become progressives by adopting Han ways; some had begun successful careers but wanted greater opportunities to assert their Uyghur identity.[3]

Studies and analysis of Uyghurs in mostly Han boarding schools outside of Xinjiang (which were founded in 2000) and another study about their lives in college reveal a similarly mixed picture.[4] The Uyghurs in the boarding schools realized that they had been granted opportunities that would shape their careers and lives. They could aspire to higher positions in government, the economy, or society. Other than teaching the Uyghur students in the Chinese language and improving their skills and competence, the government planned to use these schools to promote ethnic integration and political goals, which included positive attitudes toward Communism and China. Such efforts were no doubt part of the government's objective, which included an emphasis on speaking Chinese and refraining from expression of Islamic beliefs and practices. Teachers worked closely with students not simply on academics but in their personal lives.

The schools, on occasion, fell short because of the cultural divide between the Han and the Uyghurs. For example, the Uyghur girls favored colorful clothing and scarves and wore makeup whereas the Han girls did not apply makeup and perhaps found it distasteful. Although the Uyghur students were discouraged from religious and cultural expression, they found ways of identifying themselves (wearing skull caps, playing on the same football teams, etc.) as Uyghurs and Muslims.

Similarly, integration on the college level did not fulfill the PRC's objective. Han and Uyghurs lived in separate dormitories, partly due to distinctive diets but also because of different curricula. The Uyghurs studied the Chinese language whereas the Han studied English, not Uyghur. The Uyghurs believed that the Han in Xinjiang insulted them by not attempting to learn Uyghur, the language of 50 percent of the region's population. Stereotypes about the Other persisted. Some Han believed that the Uyghurs were less capable, whereas some Uyghurs found the Han to be unclean. Uyghur students often congregated together, and the Han students also met together. They often played apart, with Uyghurs and Han practicing soccer by themselves.[5] Timothy Grose, who studied these schools, argued that most of the Uyghurs he interviewed became more assertive about their identities (clothing, music, Islam, etc.).

The government would point to the advantages of the boarding schools. It noted that the children received a quality education and were provided with excellent medical care. It also asserted that the graduates achieved a higher standard of living because of the superior education in the boarding schools, and critics have acknowledged that often to be the case. The education in the boarding schools was superior to the schools in Xinjiang, and many Uyghur parents agreed. In 2017, 43,000 students, mostly Uyghurs, applied for the 9,880 places in the schools.[6] On the other hand, critics charged that the career prospects of the graduates if they returned to Xinjiang were frequently limited to teaching or serving as bank clerks, police officers, or other low-level jobs, partly due to Han employers' reluctance to hire Uyghurs. Thus, some Uyghurs attempted to avoid a return to Xinjiang and sought employment in central China. Grose concludes that discrimination against educated Uyghurs is likely, but the government has not issued statistical breakdowns of employment for Uyghurs.[7]

UYGHUR DISSATISFACTION AND PRC RESPONSES

Unsettled conditions and perhaps less favorable career prospects led some Uyghurs to seek solace in alcohol and drugs. Afghanistan, which shares a common border with Xinjiang, offered a ready supply of heroin. The PRC has remained secretive about the number of addicts, especially among the Uyghur population. Similarly, it has not revealed the number of Uyghurs afflicted by HIV-AIDS through the sharing of infected needles. No doubt, prostitution contributed to the spread of HIV-AIDS, but statistics on the incidence of the disease are limited. Reports have surfaced that *mäshräp* meetings tried to work with addicts, but the government feared organizations that it did not control, particularly those with a religious link, and limited such meetings.

The government nonetheless persisted in its policy of rewards and punishment for much of the decade starting in 2000. It sought, for example, to create a Uyghur middle class through economic growth. The success of such a policy would ingratiate the government to this new and more prosperous community. Pursuing such an agenda, the government would not focus on issues of social class. Socialist ideology would be relegated to a lesser position than improving the life of this hoped-for burgeoning middle class. Many merchants who were involved in cross-border trade with Central Asia and Pakistan often did well and would provide one part of this new middle class. Education would, in theory, help make Uyghurs and other non-Han eligible for the professions or business. The result would be reduction of economic inequality between Han and non-Han. Another strategy for development in Xinjiang was the Paired Assistance Program, a policy of linking so-called advanced regions to so-called less advanced regions (*duikuo zhiyuan*), with the former assisting the latter, and thus Xinjiang receiving the help of other regions. However, until 2010, the northeast Chinese province of Shandong was Xinjiang's only provider of such aid.

Another way the PRC and the Communist Party attempted to ingratiate themselves with the Uyghurs was to increase the number of non-Han cadres, a position that provided status and economic advantages. Starting in 2004, the Communist Party added more minority cadres. One supplementary benefit for the party was that cadres could not have religious beliefs, undercutting the overt expression of Islam. The government also encouraged educated non-Han to move to cities, perhaps hoping, in this way, to undermine their identities with specific localities, families, and ethnicities, although economic motivations, the need for more workers in the urban areas, may have been the prime motivation. These efforts bore some fruit. A Uyghur and non-Han middle class began to develop in business and the professions. Some Uyghurs organized the same kind of networks, known to the Han as *guanxi* (relationships), with other Uyghurs, as well as with Han, and prospered.

Joanne Smith Finley reported that a survey conducted in 2000 found that 78 percent of Han approved of intermarriages with Uyghurs, but only 33 percent of Uyghurs did so.[8] The government sought to encourage intermarriages by providing better housing and other perks for such couples,[9] and a few Uyghur women actually had positive views about Han men. Asserting that some Uyghur men abused their wives, they began to marry Han men. Some resented the Islamic practice of *talaq*, by which men could secure a divorce simply by announcing it three times, which resulted in one of the highest divorce rates in the country; some appreciated civil registration of marriage, which offered them legal protection. Other reasons Uyghur women gave for intermarriage was "the desire to avoid [Uyghur] chauvinism" and "the desire to improve socioeconomic status."[10] Yet intermarriages remained few and far between. The situation in the Inner Mongolian Autonomous Region differed, as Han and Mongolian intermarriages had been increasing at a rapid clip. Religion was not an impediment in such intermarriages. Moreover, Mongolians constituted less than 20 percent of the Inner Mongolian population, while Uyghurs comprised almost 50 percent of the population in Xinjiang, allowing them greater flexibility in mate selection.

Other developments were less positive. A 2006 study found that Uyghurs had a higher rate of poverty and were less healthy than the Han. Uyghurs had lower-paying jobs, and even Uyghurs who knew Chinese did not have the type of employment commensurate with their skills. The less skilled Uyghurs worked in lower-level positions; even in farming, they often had less fertile land.[11] Divisions among the non-Han contributed to additional problems; such divisions led to instability in Xinjiang. Uyghurs in Yining, for example, asserted that the Kazakhs received the best employment, causing friction among the two groups. The non-Han also resented the government's environmental policies. Support for sometimes indiscriminate logging led to deforestation. Substantial increases in population also generated problems—for example, the Han in-migration infringed upon the survival of wildlife; and the extraction of minerals and oil resulted in less water for and damage to the land for herders and farmers.

Because the government remained concerned about Islam, it continued to impose limitations on the religion. It oversaw the training of and licensing of imams, reduced the number of newly constructed mosques, disapproved of religious services in the home, and banned certain religious publications. It appeared more concerned about Islam among the Uyghurs than among the Kazakhs, many of whom were pastoral nomads and did not construct many mosques. Yet the lack of religious buildings did not necessarily translate into less religious feelings. The government seemed to condone excesses in proscriptions on Islam. Muslims were pressured to eat during the day in the month of Ramadan, a major taboo. Women wearing veils and men with beards were, on occasion, harassed by security forces.

The government feared, in particular, intellectuals who reputedly gave an impetus to ethnic "separatism" by emphasizing Uyghur history or who covertly criticized Chinese policies. In 2005, the leadership interpreted a story, which was published in Kashgar, by a poet and short-story writer, Nurmemet Yasin, as a satirical critique of the government's attitudes toward Uyghurs. The writer was arrested, found guilty of "inciting separatism," and sentenced to ten years in prison, where he died at the age of thirty-four. This effort spread to Uyghur books and folk songs and concerts, which were subject to censorship, if they were deemed to have "splittist" or "separatist" contents. Police forces, on occasion, searched for contraband, which, in this case, meant books or journals depicted as subversive. Uyghurs or other non-Han harboring such contraband items could be arrested, and the number of those arrested increased throughout the early 2000s. The PRC's concerns about critical books even spread to the United States. About fifteen foreign specialists on the Uyghurs contributed essays to a volume titled *Xinjiang: China's Muslim Borderland*, which was edited by S. Frederick Starr and published in 2004. Several of the articles were critical of Chinese government policy in Xinjiang, which irritated PRC leaders. The government condemned the book, which would otherwise not have reached a wide audience, and rejected visa applications from the authors whose inability to visit China impeded their careers. This action made the government vulnerable to numerous accusations of censorship.

Despite these cultural issues and just complaints about government censorship, Xinjiang witnessed significant economic growth during the first decade of the twenty-first century. The Chinese strategy of economic gains for the non-Han leading to peace, which would eventually result in harmonious relations between the Han and the non-Han, appeared to be successful. The living standards of most inhabitants in Xinjiang rose. Oases or small towns grew into large centers or cities, with good roads and housing. The life span of the principal non-Chinese groups increased, with the Kazakhs jumping from 67.42 years in 2000 to 72.35 years in 2010 and the Uyghurs from 67.44 years to 72.37 years during the same period, as a result of better medical and hygienic facilities. Non-Han children also had a better student-to-teacher ratio in their ethnic schools, with the Kazakhs having one teacher for 14.21 students and the Han having one teacher for every 17.67 students.

Cessation of nuclear tests removed a central grievance of the non-Han. Xinjiang was no longer the site of nuclear testing, although the disposal of nuclear waste and other environmental problems still remained. Few violent incidents were recorded, although the government arrested several thousand non-Han for expressions of "splittism," or extremism. The fundamentalist violence that had spread through much of the Islamic world seemed to have missed Xinjiang. Economic growth lifted the living standards of most inhabitants of Xinjiang, including the non-Han.

Nonetheless, some Uyghurs and non-Han continued to have stereotypes about the Han. They asserted that the Han did not eat sufficient quantities of meat and were thus neither strong nor athletic, and they complained that the Han ate everything, even the most disgusting creatures. They were repelled by the dirtiness, the spitting in the streets, and the smoking and excessive drinking they attributed to the Han. They proudly distinguished between Uyghur women who wore colorful dresses and were curvaceous and the Han women who allegedly wore drab outfits and did not have voluptuous figures. Finally, they claimed that the Han were not as joyous as the non-Han, who loved to sing and dance. On the other hand, some Han persisted in their stereotypes that Uyghurs were backward, lazy, and dirty. All these complaints translated into a lack of socialization among Chinese and Uyghurs. Uyghurs also resented the fact that Uyghur and non-Chinese publications were limited. For example, the number of children's books written in Chinese in circulation amounted to 16,848 while the children's books in Uyghur came to a paltry 134.

VIOLENT EXPLOSIONS

Under these circumstances, the violence in Urumchi in 2009 was a major shock. In fact, James Millward, one of the most distinguished specialists on the Uyghurs, and other students of Xinjiang had written a few years before 2009 that violence had been receding since 1997–1998.[12] They also suggested that most of the violence reflected local conflicts rather than planned actions of Uyghur splittists, or extremists.[13] Other incidents had preceded the chaos in Urumchi, but none had the same impact as the conflagration in Xinjiang's capital.

The government had, on several occasions, publicized police or army raids that had captured or killed Islamic fundamentalists. It had also pointed to the Turkistan Islamic Party (or TIP), a descendant of the Eastern Turkistan Islamic Movement (or ETIM), as a terrorist group supported by the Taliban and al-Qaeda. Based in Waziristan, Pakistan, TIP began to issue videos (some on the internet) urging Uyghurs to initiate a jihad in Xinjiang. The videos also warned foreigners not to participate in the Olympics in Beijing in 2008, which the PRC was proud to host. Whether the TIP was cohesive or a true threat, its videos frightened many Han settlers in Xinjiang and was a potential threat to the government.[14] PRC leaders had been determined to use the Olympics to emphasize China's stability, security, and successes to the rest of the world. The TIP's threats thus were taken seriously, and an attack on the police in Kashgar in August of the Olympic year, which led to the deaths of eighteen policemen, confirmed the PRC's fears. Shortly thereafter, a group of Uyghurs attacked a police station in the city of Kucha in southern Xinjiang. The government sought to explain away these attacks by noting that both cities were predominantly Uyghur or sympathetic to Uyghurs and had a small contingent of radical Islamic fundamentalists and "splittists."

Urumchi differed from Kashgar and Kucha because it had become an increasingly Han majority city. Nonetheless, Urumchi also had some Uyghur migrants who had been unemployed and had few prospects and others who aspired to careers and a better life within the existing system. They faced competition from Han workers for employment in construction, a booming part of the economy as the city continued to attract both Han migrants from other parts of China and Uyghurs and non-Han from southern Xinjiang. The more skilled and educated Uyghur migrants were frustrated by the favorable opportunities for the Han in the city, but they persevered, and indeed a few succeeded and became part of the middle and professional classes.

The arrival of Han and Uyghur migrants had proceeded peacefully until 2009, when an incident as far away as possible from the city led to violence. Since 2000, the government had encouraged the pairing of so-called backward Xinjiang with allegedly more advanced provinces. The tangible results were opportunities for Uyghur students to attend boarding schools and for

Uyghur adults to work in factories in distant areas. The government had transferred tens of thousands of Uyghurs, mostly women, to work in the more prosperous factories along the eastern coast.

A toy factory in Shaoguan in Guangdong province had recruited two hundred Uyghurs from Kashgar, which entailed a sizable trek from northwest to southeast China. Representing only about 1 percent of the factory's workforce, they lived in separate dormitories, partly because they were not fluent in Chinese, but also because of different diets, clothing, and lifestyles from the Han workers. In May of 2009, trouble erupted. Word spread that six Uyghurs had raped two Han women, a false accusation for which several of the Han perpetrators would eventually be given the death penalty and another would be arrested. On June 29, incensed by this inaccurate claim, Han workers confronted Uyghurs, killing two of them, and the subsequent demonstrations and conflagrations resulted in more than a hundred injuries.

News and images of the incident reached Xinjiang and aroused some Uyghurs. On July 5, an event that became known as 7/5, Uyghurs demonstrated on the streets of Urumchi at the big market, and some in the crowd attacked Han stores and businesses, as well as individual Han. Numerous buildings and vehicles were destroyed. Few of the Uyghurs were intent on violence, and many demonstrators had intended to protest peacefully and had helped some Han to escape from marauders. Yet the violent demonstrators prevailed and went on a killing spree; it was not a peaceful protest, judging from the fact that most of the casualties were Han.[15] Police and army units, with tasers, water hoses, tear gas, and guns, had to be called in to end the disturbances. Two days later, Han appeared on the streets, and clashes erupted between them and Uyghurs, leading to several deaths. PRC sources reported that 197 Han and non-Han, but mostly Han, had been killed during these events. Over the next week, the authorities cut off internet and other communications in Xinjiang, preventing independent observers from gauging the accuracy of these statistics. Urumchi remained tense for some time.

A few months later, Han inhabitants complained that Uyghurs, carrying syringes, had attacked them without any provocation. Some of these reports of attacks appeared to be hysterical reactions, as doctors noticed that the wounds were not caused by needles. Han inhabitants blamed Wang Lequan, who had been secretary of the Communist Party in Xinjiang since 1994, for not "striking hard" against Islamic radicals. In September, Han residents of the city and perhaps some outsiders led demonstrations to protest against what they perceived to be government inaction, and the police had to be called upon to quell the disturbances, which resulted in five deaths. The Uyghurs, in turn, complained that the police and army were slow in protecting them. The authorities in Xinjiang attempted to challenge that perception, noting that the state would protect both Han and Uyghurs.

The government blamed outside agitators for the demonstrations and pointed, in particular, to Rebiya Kadeer for instigating violence. The authorities asserted that she communicated with the leaders of the demonstration and encouraged them to attack the Han. She responded that she had called to encourage her brother not to leave his house and to refrain from joining the demonstrations.

Most important, the Urumchi clashes initiated a partial reversal in the government's carrots and sticks policy. Here is the government's viewpoint: PRC leaders asserted that they had devoted considerable efforts and resources to foster development in Xinjiang to improve the lives of the Uyghurs. They initiated affirmative action policies designed to assist the non-Han in education, employment, and careers. They argued that their policy of development of the Western regions of China, starting in the late

1990s, had benefited Xinjiang. Although the non-Han had still not reached the same economic levels as the Han, their lifestyles and their health had improved. The government emphasized that it had recruited Uyghurs and Kazakhs as Communist Party cadres, offering them leadership positions in society. It also had improved the standards at Xinjiang University in Urumchi—certainly as compared to Doak Barnett's description of Xinjiang College, as it was known in 1948. Its economic leaders and consultants had fostered cotton cultivation, leading to impressive gains in production; had discovered and helped to extract mineral and natural resources in Xinjiang; had introduced new technologies; and had promoted industrialization. It had built roads, railway tracks, and airports to link Xinjiang with China, as well as with Central Asia, providing greater access to markets for products from Xinjiang.

The lives of ordinary Uyghurs and non-Han had, in fact, improved. Their incomes had increased, and they had labor-saving appliances. As of the 2010 census, 96.1 per 100 Uyghur households had washing machines; the comparable figure for Han was 97.12; 94.35 per 100 Uyghur households had refrigerators; 96.84 Han had refrigerators. 76.59 per Uyghur households had water heaters for showers while 88.97 Han had such water heaters.[16] The discrepancy between the Han and the Uyghurs in ownership of such appliances was slight, but the Han regions had about a fifteen-year advantage in the onset of economic growth. Health and education statistics also confirm rapid progress in Xinjiang. Doak Barnett's 1948 report on Xinjiang, as well as those of other travelers in Xinjiang in the 1940s, offered a devastating portrait of poverty, backwardness, a Xinjiang college that was "clownish," an exploitative elite, and inadequate educational and medical facilities contrasted sharply with the Xinjiang of the early twenty-first century, which the PRC had created.[17] The government also stated that it had eliminated some of the traditional restrictions on non-

Han women, allowing them to play political and economic roles and, in some cases, to rise in leadership positions.

These views were naturally one-sided and did not emphasize some of the negative, repressive, or discriminatory policies the PRC had pursued. Yet many Han believed in these perceptions and considered some of the non-Han to be ungrateful for the benefits they had received from Communist rule.

Even after years of living in the same cities and regions, quite a few Uyghurs and the Han persisted in stereotypes about the other. Some, but not all, Uyghurs responded with problems they had described earlier but added new ones. They asserted, with some justification, that Han workers received more subsidies and that the arrival of Han farmers, often in collective farms supported by the *bingtuan*, in Xinjiang, had undercut Uyghur farmers and had strained water resources and depleted the forests. Similarly, the government's drilling for oil and extracting of mineral resources had resulted in expropriation of Uyghur farms and endangered the aquifers. They complained that in the process of rapid urbanization, Han and elite Uyghurs had coopted land that previously had served as bazaars or Muslim cemeteries or had been earlier granted to mosques. Moreover, non-Han people and institutions had not received sufficient compensation. In addition, some non-Han resented the limits the government imposed on the expression of their religion and cultural heritage, including their music and their literature, and on restrictions on women's ability to wear veils and head scarves and on men's sporting of beards and wearing of skull caps (or *doppas*). Perhaps the most significant critique was the lack of control or input on decision making concerning Xinjiang. They asserted that the levers of power remained in the hands of the Han.

As in the past, many Han portrayed the Uyghurs as lazy and uninterested in improving their economic prospects by learning

Chinese. They depicted the Uyghurs as almost childlike in their love of song and dance and feasts. Yet the Han added a new and more sinister portrait of the Uyghurs. The violent incidents in Xinjiang now prompted the Han to conjure an image of Uyghurs as dangerous, and ordinary Han were advised to be on their guard when they were near Uyghurs.

The presentation of these starkly different perceptions should not be construed as a portrait of monolithic Han and non-Han views. Some Uyghurs had profited from government investment starting in the 1990s and formed a middle class, with a few rich individuals, while some, who were engaged in agriculture, herding, or in relatively unskilled urban jobs, were not as satisfied with the PRC. Their differing economic statuses would shape their attitudes toward the Han and the government. The middle class appears not to have been as opposed to Han rule as those who had not achieved that status. On the other side, some Han believed that the government had been heavy-handed in its policies toward the Uyghurs and hoped that the PRC would adopt more moderate policies toward the non-Han.

Divisions and differences in attitudes among the Han, who were not all monolithic, were based on the times of their migrations to Xinjiang. Many of the Old Han, who moved due to government pressure before the late 1990s, were part of the *bingtuan*. They worked in state farms or factories or other enterprises and received decent wages and benefits. Most of the New Han, who were attracted to Xinjiang by government support of and investment in the region starting in the late 1990s, often worked in the extractive or energy industries. The New Han had greater economic opportunities and benefits. For example, the China National Petroleum Company offered higher wages and greater benefits and provided housing, schools, hospitals, and recreational and entertainment facilities in newly rebuilt towns where it had demolished old structures and constructed imposing steel buildings. It was only natural that the Old Han would resent the perks that the New Han enjoyed.

PEACE THROUGH MODERATION OR STRIKE HARD POLICIES?

The government's new restrictive policies began immediately after the pacification of the Urumchi disturbances. Police and army forces sought out and arrested more than a thousand people whom the government labeled terrorists. Rumors about beatings of those arrested circulated among the Uyghur population, though it was difficult to confirm these reports. Within a few months, the government executed more than twenty Uyghurs, and at least one received a punishment of life imprisonment. The government then temporarily closed mosques in the city. Surveillance in Xinjiang increased dramatically and would be even more pervasive in the decade of the 2010s. Police and army, with considerable firepower, were stationed throughout the major cities, particularly in central areas or in the principal squares. The government suspended internet access in Xinjiang for about six months after the Urumchi riots, exhibiting its view that outside agitators had precipitated the violence, and it banned nongovernmental organizations.

The government hardliners, as well as the non-Han extremists, dominated events for the next few years, but ordinary Uyghurs and Han were also affected. Together with the violence, such nonviolent assertions as jokes and songs appeared among ordinary people, who also showed greater interest in Uyghur history and heritage. Uyghur competition with newly arriving Han workers in education, employment, and wages exacerbated tensions, which also led to assertions of the Islamic heritage, including an increase in pilgrimages to Sufi saints' tombs. At the same time, fundamentalist Islam became more popular among the minority of extremists, prompting state officials to be wary of any form of the religion.

After the violence in Urumchi, the government also sought policies to foster stability. By 2014, it had transferred approximately ten thousand non-Han children from Xinjiang to the central provinces of China and enrolled them in better schools than were found in their native lands. Despite the contretemps in the Guangzhou factory that reverberated and led directly to the violence in Urumchi, the government continued the policy of transferring Uyghur workers, mostly to eastern China, believing that better economic conditions would translate into less tension and violence. The Uyghurs would earn higher wages in the central part of China than in Xinjiang and would presumably be reluctant to support antigovernment activities. The PRC leaders assumed that economic development would be a panacea.

One major carrot was a meeting of major leaders in a Xinjiang Work Forum in May of 2010. The forum concluded that the government would place greater emphasis on the Partnership Assistance Program, increasing the number of such projects to about twenty by 2020. Provinces throughout China linked up with specific cities or regions in Xinjiang to offer financial assistance, expertise on economic development, and investment. They also donated books, helped in extraction of minerals, and promoted tourism. These efforts were eventually designed to create a harmonious society (*hexie shehui*). The prosperous cities would be expected to serve as mentors for the towns and rural regions in Xinjiang and to dispatch technical experts, known as *rencai*, who were granted bonuses and rewards, to assist the local economies.

Xinjiang's provincial or urban partners from east China would also supply a portion of their GDP as capital for industrial development and would provide funds for health care and social welfare. The most important such link would be between Shenzhen, the prosperous free trade zone on the east coast, and Kashgar, which would lay the foundation for industrial growth in the city. As part of this development policy, the government provided greater support for applied science and technology in schools and universities in Xinjiang. It asserted that it expended considerable income in Xinjiang, for which the region's inhabitants should be grateful instead of complaining about the environmental damage that mining and industry wrought. Yet some provinces in the central and eastern regions of China, inhabited by Han, apparently resented the additional economic burdens of supplying such investment and expertise.

The Xinjiang Work Forum also pledged increased revenue for Xinjiang. A higher proportion of the taxes imposed on Xinjiang's energy resources, which amounted to 15 percent of the oil and 25 percent of the natural gas in the country, would be granted to the region. New industrial enterprises in Kashgar would receive a two-year tax holiday. The government also pledged to bolster the economies of the southern and eastern regions of Xinjiang, the principal habitats of the Uyghurs. It also committed itself to increasing wages and offering unemployment insurance in those areas, to increasing the stipends of non-Han students in boarding schools, and to offering more bilingual education for non-Han students.

In April of 2010, the government's appointment of Zhang Chunxian as the replacement for Wang Lequan as secretary of the Chinese Communist Party and the leader of the *bingtuan* was another attempt to win over the population. Wang had alienated both the Uyghurs and the Han. He had been associated with the Strike Hard policies, which had imposed harsh punishments on Uyghur dissenters and not merely on perpetrators of violence. At the same time, the Han did not believe that Wang had protected them from the riots in Urumchi and the subsequent syringe attacks. Corruption in the government also contributed to popular Chinese dissatisfaction with Wang. Rumors spread that Wang was an alcoholic and had been drunk on the day of the violence. On the other hand, Zhang pledged to promote economic development. He emphasized industrial growth; construction of bridges and roads; establishment of a special economic zone in Kashgar; restoration of tourism, which had decreased due to the violence; and catering to the huge Han markets in other provinces. He also restored the internet and telephone connections that had been severed after the riots in Urumchi. Perhaps as important, he initiated campaigns against corruption in government and the Communist Party. For example, he eliminated grandiose banquets and other perks for officials.

Another policy entailed alterations in Kashgar. Asserting that the city's old buildings were not earthquake-proof and lacked modern conveniences, the government razed much of the old town. Thousands of homes were destroyed, and more than 50,000 households and 200,000 people were moved, with some transferred as much as ten kilometers distant from their old neighborhoods. Modern-style apartment buildings were rapidly constructed for the dispossessed tenants. The traditional and renowned Id Kah mosque was not touched. The government may have viewed these renovations and reconstructions as upgrades for Kashgar's inhabitants, who were allegedly receiving safer residences with modern appliances and conveniences.

Yet critics proposed a different motive for the government's policy. They claimed that the government sought to subvert Uyghur identity by targeting traditional neighborhoods and lifestyles. By moving Uyghurs and other non-Han into nondescript modern buildings and in the same areas as the Han, the government reputedly attempted to subvert Uyghur traditions and identity and to promote intermarriage. This particular accusation against the government appears to be overstated. The destruction of old structures and so-called *hutong*, or alleyways, and the construction of new apartment buildings and offices had been policies pursued throughout China, including Beijing, Hangzhou, and other cities on China's east coast. The same kind of accusation had been leveled at Georges-Eugène Haussmann, who destroyed medieval sections of Paris from 1852 to 1870 and built wide avenues and parks. Critics can lament the destruction of ancient structures, but implying that such policies were exclusively designed to undermine a particular culture is another matter. Without additional evidence, it would be difficult to confirm the critics' views that the razing of old buildings in Kashgar deliberately targeted Uyghur attempts to preserve their identities. Another, and possibly likelier, explanation is that new construction was profitable for builders and banks.

The government also initiated policies associated with the "stick" as opposed to the "carrot." The harsher policies entailed heightened security in public transport, greater visibility of police and army, closer supervision of the internet and overseas telephone calls, and the use of hidden cameras. If the authorities found evidence of discussion of what they labeled separatism or fundamentalism, they would act to suppress such expressions. Even if these views derived from outside of China, they would seek to ban them. For example, the government attempted but failed to prevent the showing of a generally positive documentary about Rebiya Kadeer in Australia. It also kept close tabs on the communications and daily lives of non-Han who had relatives abroad and tried to persuade the Central Asian countries and Turkey, which had communities of Uyghurs, to monitor dissident activities.

Some non-Han condemned other policies instituted after the Urumchi disturbances of 2009. They resented the 2010 imposition of Chinese as the sole language of instruction in secondary schools, which deprived Uyghurs of the study of their own culture. Indeed, more and more Uyghurs could not read the classics of Uyghur literature. As early as 2002, instruction in Chinese was mandated in Xinjiang University. A few non-Han students also resented impediments to study abroad and claimed that the Han who wished to do so did not face the same stumbling blocks. They also complained that those Uyghurs and non-Han who were fortunate enough to be recruited as Communist Party cadres, a plum opportunity, were given the appalling task of announcing and often enforcing the most unpopular laws or rules.

Critics of the government were also concerned about restrictions on the size of families. The one child per family regulations had not initially been applied to the non-Han, but Uyghurs feared that that they would be subject to these limitations. Facing this possibility, they devised strategies to evade such regulations. For example, a third or fourth child in a family might be turned over to and reared by relatives or childless women.

Violence persisted in the years after the Urumchi riots of 2009. In August of 2010, Uyghurs set off a bomb in Aksu, which killed seven people and injured fourteen. On July 18, 2011, Uyghur militants raided a police station in Khotan, which was followed later in the month by an attack in Kashgar. The government blamed terrorists and separatists for this violence, and indeed at least one of the militants had been trained in Waziristan, but some Uyghurs attributed the attacks to local antagonisms. Sporadic outbreaks erupted throughout 2012 and 2013, including an attack in Yecheng, a town on the border with Pakistan, leading to fifteen deaths, an abortive attempt to hijack an airline, continued raids on police stations, and an attack in Bachu, during which twenty-one died; quite a number of such incidents took place in 2013–2014. The government responded with executions, imprisonments, and tighter security. The most dramatic and influential incident occurred in Tiananmen Square. On October 28, 2013, a car with three Uyghurs attempted to run down pedestrians in this central location in Beijing. The incident culminated in a fiery crash, killing two and injuring thirty-eight others. A militant Uyghur organization claimed responsibility for this grisly event. It wanted to make a great impression with a spectacular incident, and the government clearly paid attention.

XI JINPING AND THREE NEW POLICIES

Xi Jinping was affected by this Tiananmen incident. He had just been proclaimed general secretary of the Chinese Communist Party on November 15, 2012, and president of the PRC on March 14, 2013. Tiananmen was right where the leadership lived and worked, and Xi was determined to respond to the violent attack in that square. He needed a safe and peaceful Xinjiang to embark on his three most significant objectives: trade with Central Asia, extraction of Xinjiang's natural resources, and the Belt and Road Initiative. Unlike other earlier leaders, he appeared less interested in winning over the Uyghurs' hearts and minds than in securing his goals.

Xi, the son of an early and powerful Communist leader, would eventually seek to promote China's new and more assertive presence on the world stage. Early in his career, a year before the start of the Cultural Revolution in 1966, his father had been purged; and shortly thereafter, the authorities sent Jinping to a remote area, where he lived in a cave. He was eventually released and earned a degree in chemical engineering, but he opted for a career in politics and was extraordinarily successful.[18] As head of state and the Communist Party, as well as chair of the Military Commission, he sought the limelight, consolidated power, and abandoned the collective leadership that had developed after Mao Zedong's death. He sought to avert the fate of the USSR, which had collapsed in the early 1990s, and he was eager to secure the respect due China as the world's second greatest economic power.

Like earlier Communist Party leaders, Xi first sought an increase in trade with Central Asia, an objective that related to Xinjiang. The opening of a pipeline from Kazakhstan to China in 2005 had offered a reliable source of oil, but the pipeline crossed Xinjiang, a possible security risk because of the tension and violence in the region. Xinjiang needed to be secure if China wished to maintain trade with Central Asia.

China repeatedly dispatched goods to Kyrgyzstan and Tajikistan but faced difficulties in economic relations with other Central Asian areas. Because Kyrgyzstan and Tajikistan bordered on China, Chinese goods could readily be transported there. China encountered problems in other regions. Trucks and trains with trade products were often delayed on the borders, as some customs officials demanded bribes; the infrastructure in Central Asia was rudimentary; governments imposed high tariffs; and border areas were often afflicted by drug and human trafficking and livestock theft, among other impediments.

The establishment of two towns named Khorgos, one on the Chinese side of the border and the other on the border of Kazakhstan, as free economic zones was designed to overcome these difficulties. In Xi's first year, a train from Urumchi to Khorgos was completed, linking Xinjiang to Khorgos. A pipeline had also been constructed from Kazakhstan to China. The two "Khorgoses" became significant industrial centers, with growing populations and apparently prosperous economies. Corruption, in the form of smuggling and the cupidity of customs officials, persisted, but the two towns witnessed economic growth. The key to future success was a peaceful and stable Xinjiang. If disruptions and violence plagued Xinjiang, Xi's plans for Central Asian trade and for contact between China and Kazakhstan would be hampered. An additional problem for China was the large Uyghur populations in Kazakhstan and Uzbekistan, whom the PRC viewed as potential threats.

Xi's second objective involved the extraction of Xinjiang's own natural resources. Non-Han and some Han had already complained about the environmental damage that mining and oil drilling on lands that had significant numbers of non-Han caused. As noted earlier, Uyghurs had also asserted that the government's emphasis on cotton cultivation had depleted the water supply and that the in-migration of Han peasants had, in addition, impinged upon the forests and the water in the region. Despite such concerns, Xi and the government were intent on the drilling of oil and gas in the town of Karame, which provided 40 percent of the domestic consumption of gas, and in Korla. The China National Petroleum Company controlled the oil resources, and the leaders of the company were often at least as powerful as the local governments. Drilling for oil, which required quite a few experts, resulted in the arrival of more Han, which irritated some Uyghurs. Workers in Karame endured difficult circumstances, but the pay compensated for such a demanding life. In Korla, workers were rewarded with high salaries and some free food, as well as with good schools and hospitals. The arrangement was paternalistic, but the workers still benefited.

The Han workers in the *bingtuan* who had built the infrastructure of roads, canals, and railroads that provided access to the oil and gas fields did not fare as well. Their wages were lower than the ones for the workers in the oil and gas fields or in the offices of the Tarim Oil Company, which was placed in charge, and their other benefits were more limited than those of the new arrivals. The animosities between the Old Han settlers in the *bingtuan* and the new Han added to the difficulties in Xinjiang. Naturally, a peaceful and stable Xinjiang was essential for China's ability to access the area's abundant resources.

Xi's last objective was his One Belt One Road initiative (renamed Belt and Road Initiative in 2016), which he announced in 2013 during visits to Kazakhstan and Indonesia. This ambitious project referred to the land-based and maritime routes that linked China to Central, South, and Southeast Asia and the Middle East. The "Belt" designated the caravan routes of the Silk Roads, while the "Road" meant the maritime routes to Southeast, South, and West Asia. The China Infrastructure Investment Bank and the Silk Roads Bank, with an initial fund of $40 billion for these projects, would provide loans and grants estimated at $4 to $8 trillion over the decades. The initiative had a breathtaking range from China to Russia to Central Asia to Siberia to South, Southeast, and West Asia to Europe to Africa.

Of the projects, three were relevant to Xinjiang. The North Belt or the Eurasian Land Bridge stretched from China through Kazakhstan to Central Asia to Europe; the Central Asia Belt covered Xinjiang, Central Asia, West Asia, the Persian Gulf, Turkey, and the Mediterranean Sea; and the China Pakistan Economic Corridor included Xinjiang and Pakistan. Roads and high-speed railroads would be built that would reduce the travel time for goods from China to Europe, creating a Eurasian Land Bridge. Dams, power grids, and airports would also be constructed. Some projects, such as construction of a subway in Belgrade, elevated rail in Bogota, a telecom and data system in Nairobi, and a shopping center in Georgia, have gone beyond these original plans. Xi also emphasized that such cultural and educational exchanges as art exhibits would accompany the economic ones and would be as significant. Naturally, Chinese loans and actual construction projects could translate into influence over its partners in these initiatives.

In addition to the environmental stumbling blocks such as deserts, avalanches, and lofty mountains, the unstable regions in Central Asia, Pakistan, and West Asia also posed serious difficulties for the Belt and Road Initiative. Critics have also complained that environmental issues had not been considered. They asserted that infrastructure projects often translated into degradation of land and siphoning of water reserves from peasants and herders. They argued that corruption was almost endemic in such grandiose infrastructure projects. Finally, some foreigners accused the PRC of seeking to trap governments into accepting loans that these countries could not repay, thus giving China considerable leverage over them. Whatever the criticism, a stable Xinjiang was essential for Xi's projects.

The ensuing two years after Xi's announcement of the One Belt One Road initiative were filled with violence in Xinjiang. In June of 2013, militants killed fifteen and injured fifty in Khotan in protests against the closing of a mosque and imprisonment of an imam. The government responded by executing the three men involved in the incident and mandating life imprisonment for the woman. On July 30, 2014, three militants assassinated Jüme Tahir, vice president of the Chinese Islamic Association and the imam of the Id Kah mosque, perhaps the most renowned in the country, in Kashgar. They viewed him as a collaborator with the PRC because he deplored violence and cooperated with the government. Many Han were shocked that the World Uyghur Congress, in Munich, did not condemn the murderers and that the Uyghur Eastern Turkistan Education and Solidarity Association, based in Turkey, supported the assassination and portrayed the assassins as heroes.

The most flamboyant incidents, which captured Xi's attention, took place outside of Xinjiang. On March 1, 2014, eight Uyghurs, in black clothing and armed with long knives, killed 31 and injured 143 at the railroad station in Kunming, a city in the southwestern province of Yunnan that had no connection with Xinjiang. On August 17, 2015, Uyghurs set off a bomb at the Erawan shrine in Bangkok, killing 20 and injuring 125. They announced that the bombing was in response to the Thai government's returning of a hundred or so Uyghur refugees to China. On July 9, 2015, disturbances erupted even in Turkey with a demonstration around the Chinese embassy in Ankara, the demonstrators protesting the PRC's reputed ban on fasting during Ramadan. Turkish police dispersed the demonstrators, and no serious injuries or deaths were reported.

XI REACTS TO VIOLENCE

Like many other Communist Party leaders, Xi apparently perceived the Uyghurs to be ungrateful for the Chinese government's strong support for economic development, greater economic equality between Han and Uyghurs, reduction of poverty among the non-Han populations, and improved medical and educational institutions instead of dependence on traditional medicine and on purely religious education. Thus, he determined on a hard line and initiated a campaign against fundamentalism, separatism, and terrorism, which he lumped together as enemies of the state. He would eventually demand even stricter censorship of the media, a Great Wall of Steel and a Great Firewall, which imposed limitations on the internet and YouTube. Restrictions and punishments, including executions for so-called fundamentalists, terrorists, and separatists, would be mandated. Xi blamed Islam, in part, for some of the violence.

The government believed that it could not tolerate the violence that erupted both in Xinjiang and China and beyond China's borders in 2014 and 2015. Many Han in Xinjiang were frightened, as may be gleaned from this dispatch by two Associated Press reporters:

> The latest attacks (May 22, 2014) have left Urumqi's ethnic (Han) Chinese on edge about their Muslim neighbors. At a convenience store on a street near the vegetable market, the operator spoke of heightened alert whenever a Uyghur steps in: "If it is a Uyghur man, we follow him in the store in case he could place something here, like an explosive."[19]

PRC leaders, including Xi, asserted that they had to act to curb the violence as expeditiously as possible, starting with limitations on religious and ethnic expressions. Thus, they renewed their ban on state employees from fasting during Ramadan, and the government often denied passports to Uyghurs seeking to travel abroad. They also insisted that Uyghurs carry identity cards listing their ethnic identities, give their children Chinese names, and, on occasion, they would not allow non-Han to register in hotels in order to prevent them from traveling. Uyghurs had to present their IDs even when buying kitchen knives. A rather unusual report, which was difficult to verify, was that the authorities compelled some Uyghur-owned stores to carry liquor, a taboo for Muslims.

Some non-Han or members of the Uyghur diaspora reported that the authorities were instructed to maintain surveillance on non-Han having contacts with foreigners or receiving phone calls from abroad or not consuming alcohol and not eating pork or frequently attending mosques. Police and army officials checked on non-Han's phones and used facial recognition technology, checkpoints, cameras and cellular towers throughout the urban areas, GPS siting of vehicles, house-to-house inspections, and DNA technology in order to ferret out "dissenters." In 2015, the government enacted a Counterterrorism Law that gave officials all these rights, as well as the opportunity to examine the work histories and bank accounts of suspects.

Communist Party cadres could check on non-Han's religious observances and many aspects of their lives. The authorities assigned specific individuals to live with non-Han in what was known as "Unite as One Family" in order to spy on and identify subversives, or "splittists." These observers looked for unauthorized videos and books, showed patriotic films, and encouraged attendance at flag-raising ceremonies. Many Uyghur families resented such intrusions on privacy rights. Policemen also conducted home inspections to ferret out dissidents and relied on neighborhood watch units (*shequ*) to report on dissenters or overly religious individuals.[20] On the other hand, in an unusual policy in August 2015, the PRC permitted Uyghurs to obtain passports in hopes that troublesome individuals would migrate to other countries, but this policy was rescinded in October 2016. It turned out that a few of the migrants joined al-Qaeda in Syria, which the PRC considered to be a threat, though the vast majority of Uyghurs simply settled in Turkey.

Government officials urged or lobbied such nearby countries as Pakistan, Afghanistan, and the Southeast Asian states, which had large fundamentalist Islamic populations, to avoid supporting "separatist" and "terrorist" Uyghurs in their own lands. There were, indeed, Uyghur extremists in those areas collaborating with local fundamentalists. A few apparently joined ISIS and al-Qaeda in the fighting in Syria, a concern for China. The Southeast Asian nations responded by sending Uyghurs back to China. Cambodia returned eighteen Uyghurs; Laos, seven; and Malaysia, thirteen. Thailand extradited more than one hundred Uyghurs, and Uyghur militants retaliated, as mentioned earlier, by attacking and killing Thais at the Erawan shrine in Bangkok. As part of the Belt and Road Initiative, the PRC had developed plans for investment in oil fields and highways in Afghanistan and a port in Pakistan. It used its economic leverage to pressure the Afghan and Pakistan governments to prevent extremists from assisting Uyghur "splittists." The government also stationed many more policemen and soldiers, often armed with considerable firepower, in Xinjiang. By 2017, there were five times more police than in 2007.

The case against Ilham Tohti epitomizes Xi's and the Chinese government's concern about and treatment of Uyghur dissidents. An economist by training, Tohti taught in Beijing, right at the center of Han political power. He first came to the attention of the authorities by setting up a website called *Uighur Online* in 2006. Uyghur expats could access and contribute to the website, which called for greater opportunities and autonomy for the non-Han inhabitants in Xinjiang. The government shut it down in 2008. Much more irritating to Han leaders was an interview Tohti gave to Radio Free Asia, one of the Communist Party's most despised organizations, in March of 2009, criticizing the government for encouraging Han to migrate to Xinjiang and for compelling Uyghur women to seek employment in the central part of China. He also enraged PRC officials by spotlighting the economic inequality between Uyghurs and Han and by calling for greater autonomy for the non-Han. Blaming him, in part, for the Urumchi riots of July 2009, the government detained him for a month but released him after considerable international pressure to do so. After his release, he continued to propose greater autonomy but not independence for Uyghurs. Yet the persistent violence and the changed environment after three major incidents in 2014, which he apparently did not condone, still put him at risk. In September of 2014, he was tried, found guilty of separatism, and sentenced to life imprisonment. This sentence reflected Xi's new policies toward the Uyghurs.

The instability and violence did not end. In 2014, an incident in Yarkand led to approximately one hundred deaths and another in Kashgar resulted in twenty-three deaths. According to some reports, in 2015, at a remote mine in Baicheng, fifty Han workers were stabbed to death. Poverty rather than association with Islamic fundamentalism, as well as resentment toward Han miners who seemed to be earning more than Uyghurs for comparable work, appeared to precipitate the incident. Ursula Gauthier, a French journalist, wrote an article blaming local authorities for this incident because of abuses and injustices leveled at the Uyghurs. She also disparaged the government's comparison of the Baicheng violence to the fundamentalists' attack on the French newspaper *Charlie Hebdo* earlier that year in Paris, claiming that the latter was an example of Islamic extremists whereas the former was not. Within a month, she was expelled from China for allegedly siding with what the government referred to as terrorists.

Another cause for concern for Xi and his government was international support for Uyghurs. For example, they asserted that Turks were apparently assisting individual Uyghurs to flee from China. In addition, Western newspapers and magazines published articles critical of Chinese Communist policy toward the Uyghurs.

Xi's objectives for the Belt and Road Initiative, development of oil resources in Xinjiang, and importation of oil and natural gas from Central Asia would be subverted unless he could pacify Xinjiang. The policies he set in place in 2014 had not ended disturbances and violence. There was considerable pressure to bring stability to Xinjiang. Eager for a resolution, Xi scanned the country to discover a solution and found Chen Quanguo, who had succeeded in generating stability in Tibet for five years. He had organized numerous "convenience police stations" throughout Tibet to monitor any untoward events and to focus on those convicted of a crime. At the same time as he implemented such tight security measures, he also emphasized economic development. Tibet had an astonishingly high GDP during his tenure. His strategies had been effective, as no violence intruded during his five-year term in Tibet. In August of 2016, Xi chose Chen to undertake the pacification of still another region—Xinjiang.

Xi and Chen had concluded that economic development alone was insufficient to achieve stability in Xinjiang and that the "virus," in Xi's words, of Islamic extremism had to be extirpated. Chen thus first placed more troops and police, allegedly as many as 90,000 security forces, again in so-called convenience police stations, in Xinjiang, especially in the south where Uyghurs were in the majority. By 2017, Xinjiang had 27 percent of the total number of arrests in the country in an area, which, by contrast, had less than 1 percent of the total population. I can attest to this increase in security personnel because I visited Yarkand, Khotan, and Kashgar a month and a half after Chen's appointment. Police, with large vehicles and powerful weapons, were stationed in the center of the cities and performed military-style drills in the main squares, which certainly appeared to be an effort to intimidate dissenters. On another occasion, three other colleagues and I were stopped in a Kashgar neighborhood outside the center, and police examined our passports for half an hour and had us call the Uyghur friend we would meet for lunch to pick us up. At another train station, a policeman asked if we were reporters because Chen's new policies entailed limitations on journalists.

By late 2017, the government began to act against specific Uyghurs. In December of that year, Rahile Dawut, a prominent Uyghur ethnographer and folklorist who taught at Xinjiang University, suddenly disappeared. The government probably detained her and would not release her, despite international protests. She had written a book on *mazars*, or shrines to local saints, at a time when the government attempted to deemphasize Uyghur culture and what it referred to as religious extremism. Perhaps government leaders viewed her as a threat due to her emphasis on Uyghur traditions and Islam.

One of the government's main objectives thus was to wean Uyghurs and non-Han away from Uyghur culture and to promote assimilation with the Han culture or a "melting pot" approach, which, they implied, had been policies in the United States and Russia. In 2017, it unveiled a new school curriculum that replaced the Uyghur language with Chinese in many courses of instruction. The leaders justified this change by noting that knowledge of Chinese was essential for Uyghur employment. Moreover, they asserted that some courses would continue to be taught in non-Han languages, and specific classes in Uyghur, Kazakh, and other languages would still be offered. Naturally, this deemphasis of Uyghur language encountered disapproval from some Uyghurs, but the Communist leaders have persisted in this policy, and, in fact, introduced a similar Chinese language curriculum in language and literature, history, and politics courses to replace native language materials in Tibet in 2018 and in Inner Mongolia in 2020, giving rise to peaceful protests.

The government also targeted Islam because Xi and other leaders were concerned about so-called religious extremism. Local officials in Xinjiang continued to inveigh against beards for men and veils for women (a policy that alienated many Uyghurs) and started even closer supervision of mosques, the training of imams, and *mazars*. Reports of a decline in attendance at mosques circulated because of reeducation and Uyghur concerns about eliciting suspicions of religious extremism.[21]

CNN reported that satellite images showed the destruction of mosques and cemeteries, focusing on a cemetery in the city of Khotan, but also mentioned quite a number of others.[22] The PRC responded that the Khotan cemetery was relocated because it was too close to residences, and children were playing there.[23] However, the authorities will not permit foreign observers in the areas of the old cemetery and the relocated graves, preventing any independent verification. In my trip to Kashgar in 2016, I visited a recently built huge two-story mosque, an indication that policies regarding Islam seemed to differ in specific neighborhoods and locations, with some areas being allowed to construct imposing mosques and other religious sites while in other regions such buildings and sites were damaged or destroyed.

Uyghurs who had relatives abroad faced scrutiny, and in a well-publicized case, a Uyghur who had been granted asylum in Belgium could not have his wife and children join him. Although both Chen and Xi directed officials, in theory, to allow Muslims to pray and to not interfere with the practice of Islam, those attending mosques or traveling to shrines or applying for travel or study abroad were often under surveillance. Many of these policies had been tried before Chen's arrival, and none had prevented the violence.

TRAINING CENTERS OR CAMPS?

The PRC now sought administrative, political, and economic control in Xinjiang. In such a large country as China, local officials had considerable authority and could, in theory, thwart or not fully carry out government initiatives. Specialists in the West have suggested that such local officials could, through delays and seemingly imperceptible alterations of instructions, undermine PRC policies. Such a scenario was probably feasible in parts of China, but Xinjiang was unique. Disorder, as well as Xinjiang's importance in Xi's plans, ensured that the central government would be actively involved in the region and would closely monitor any deviations from official policy. The new policy that Xi and Chen Quanguo now developed, and its implementation, revealed the central government's considerable authority over Xinjiang.

The newest initiative, starting in 2017, was the establishment of so-called vocational training centers, which have been labeled prison camps. Zhu Hailun, the deputy Communist Party secretary in Xinjiang, and Chen developed the plans for these camps, and the government portrayed them as centers to improve job skills, to teach the Chinese language to non-Han, and to combat religious extremism. Yet Uyghurs, Kazakhs, and Kyrgyz did not come voluntarily. Policemen and soldiers brought them to these "centers," and Xi commanded officials to detain those non-Han who, for example, had traveled abroad or sought visas or had prayed excessively. If both parents went to these "centers," children apparently were sent to boarding schools. Some reports suggest that the PRC had, in particular, targeted intellectuals and educated non-Han for these detention centers. Several Uyghurs living outside of China have stated that their relatives suddenly disappeared and were probably detained in these camps.

The government has not provided statistics for the number of detainees; some foreign observers estimate that as many as one or two million people have been detained, which would translate to anywhere from 8 to 15 percent of the Uyghur population. Because the vast majority of detainees were allegedly men of working age, about fifteen to forty-five years of age, it would appear that such disruptions would have a debilitating economic effect. Each might be in a household with two or three other people, so the spillover effect of two million in the camps might affect an unlikely number of 40 to 45 percent of the population. Many reports cite the one million figure, but we have no way to gauge the accuracy of that number. One source devised that number, based on extrapolations, several satellite images, and an increase in food, buildings, and resources in certain areas, and many newspapers and magazines have accepted that figure, but, again, it is impossible to verify.[24] The government will not provide records of those sent to camps or centers, so claims concerning the number of detainees cannot be ascertained.

The government's own instructions to camp officials, a copy of which was leaked to the *New York Times*, strongly suggest military discipline. Guards were ordered to monitor the detainees closely in classes and dormitory rooms, which were equipped with video surveillance cameras. They also needed to check people, vehicles, and goods coming into the various compound buildings throughout Xinjiang and to prevent escapes. High walls, barbed wire, and elevated guard stations that overlooked the areas enclosed the complexes. Detainees allegedly marched to military music, wore uniforms, and chanted Communist and patriotic slogans. A recent report by the US Council on Foreign Relations states that "information on what actually happens in the camps is limited," but it mentions accusations of sexual abuse and sleep deprivation. A recent account alleges that detainees could shower only once a week, women "were given one pad per day of their periods," and "one woman . . . was given only two minutes to use the toilet . . . If she took longer, she was hit with an electric baton."[25] It is difficult to verify these reports. Nonetheless, these accusations are serious enough, but critics' use of the term "concentration camps," which conjures up images of Nazi-like mass murders, may actually undercut the wider public acceptance of real abuses. There is no evidence of mass murders.

Some detainees were allegedly forced to work for extraordinarily low wages or no wages at all. Human rights organizations have referred to this as forced labor, with workers enduring brutal conditions. The factories produced consumer goods, particularly textiles, shoes, and gloves. Critics have reported that these products were sold to Western companies, which garnered considerable profits from these goods, and have lobbied for these businesses to investigate conditions in the factories. Similarly, Human Rights Watch Asia has requested investigations of labor in the countryside, including cotton farms. Several European firms have claimed that they have conducted such investigations and have not found egregious examples of forced labor. However, they have admitted that they did not have total access to factories and farms. Some human rights advocates proposed boycotts of cotton deriving from Xinjiang, which several governments, including the United States, endorse. Some manufacturers in the West have adopted a policy of checking supply lines to avoid purchasing Xinjiang cotton. PRC officials have responded that machines are used to pick 70 percent of China's cotton, and hand picking of cotton is a good-paying job and is voluntary.

One claim about the camps has proven to be false. In August of 2019, the World Bank received an accusation that some of its $50 million loan as part of its Xinjiang Technical and Vocational Education Training Project was used to pay for barbed wire, body armor, and weapons employed in the camps. The project had been designed to expand economic opportunities and to promote poverty alleviation, mostly for the Uyghurs, through assistance for vocational and technical schools. After an exhaustive study, the World Bank determined that the allegations were untrue.[26] The PRC also attempted to rebut some claims by noting that foreigners had misidentified a high school in Kashgar and an elementary school in Yantaq as reeducation camps, but it did not challenge the existence of such camps in general.[27]

The government has not permitted access to the camps by independent observers, a policy that implies that at least some of these accusations have some merit. Although some specialist teachers taught job skills and the Chinese language, numerous reports indicate that much more class time appears to have been devoted to education about Communist values and to warnings about Islamic extremism and separatism. The government seems to have attempted to transform the detainees' values, and critics have argued that it sought to have the Uyghurs and other non-Han assimilate into Chinese culture. Several former detainees have asserted that if they accepted these views or showed remorse for earlier beliefs, they would have greater chances of being released. Officials at the camps or centers would keep tabs on detainees through a scoring system. Good behavior and knowledge of adherence to the teachings in their classrooms would lead to scores that might ensure release. At the same time, if a family of a detainee did not complain and simply accepted a relative's detention, it could increase the chances for his or her release. Reports have circulated that these relatives have been stigmatized in schools and at work, with lower wages, stops at convenience police stations, checks on their IDs, and facial and DNA testing. Again, these claims are difficult to verify.

Fearful that these policies would worsen relations between Han and non-Han, some local officials sought to limit the numbers in camps and centers. However, when one such official released thousands of detainees in his area, he was dismissed, another indication of the central government's power in Xinjiang. Others, some of whom were themselves Uyghur functionaries in the camps, may have disagreed with the policies, but they carried them out. The government has responded to criticisms by pointing out that no violent incidents have been recorded in Xinjiang since the camps were established in 2017.

Xi and Chen had turned to harsh policies or "sticks." Their predecessors had relied on economic growth to achieve stability in Xinjiang. Although some Uyghurs and other non-Han had prospered and had accepted their political status as part of China, others were concerned about the potential loss of their non-Han and Islamic identities; and still others wanted to separate from China to form an independent country; and some sought an Islamic state. A few of the last group engaged in the violence that caused a crisis in China.

The government also turned to "carrots" and continued to institute affirmative action policies in education and employment, which had met with mixed success. Southern Xinjiang, where the majority of Uyghurs lived, lagged behind in employment. At various times, the authorities had permitted schools to use Uyghur as the primary language and then adopted bilingual education. As the violence did not recede, the language of instruction became Chinese. Due to the lack of dramatic success of these policies or concessions, the government concluded that extraordinary assertions of ethnic identity and of Islam had contributed to disorder and instability.

The government had earlier adopted repressive policies, especially during the Great Leap Forward of 1958 to 1962 and the Cultural Revolution of 1966 to 1976, but Xi and Chen ignored these so-called lapses and instead emphasized the economic, educational, and medical benefits China had provided for the Uyghurs and other non-Han. These allegedly benevolent policies had not prevented violence, they believed, and so they determined a reeducation of the population was required. Xi and Chen proposed changes to combat what they referred to as Islamic extremism, which allegedly required intense efforts and was used to justify the detentions and the detainees' removal from their homes. They asserted that only in a controlled environment would this reeducation succeed.

The government was also worried about the influence of Uyghurs who had traveled or lived in South Asia and the Middle

East. Even a writer sympathetic to the Uyghurs implies that the PRC ought to be concerned. In interviewing "several Uyghurs who had gained combat experience in Syria," he learned "that they are just waiting for somebody to organize a group with a viable plan to attack China."[28] Aware of such threats, the PRC leaders wanted to "inoculate" Uyghurs in China from the expat Uyghur extremists, and isolation in the camps would prevent such contacts until the trainers in the camps had transformed their "students."

At the end of the Trump administration, the US State Department labeled PRC policy in Xinjiang as genocide. J. Stapleton Roy, a former US ambassador to China who was born in China and is fluent in Chinese, sought more precision in terminology and noted, "Let's be careful with our language. Genocide is generally used to refer to the extermination of a people or nation. Genocide is not taking place. More accurately there is what can be called 'cultural genocide.'"[29] Even for some critics of PRC policies, "genocide" seems to be an overstatement. To be sure, the Uyghurs and other non-Han in the camps were involuntary detainees who were exposed to repeated lectures critical of separatism and Islamic fundamentalism. The government aimed not only to undermine "splittism," but also to have non-Han accept and appreciate the alleged benefits the PRC provided. They would learn to "love" Communism and the state. The PRC's stated objectives of teaching the Chinese language and basic vocational skills cannot be totally dismissed, but ideological changes appear to be the main goal.

The Uyghur diaspora and foreigners have accused the PRC of other human rights violations. They have claimed that the government has been attempting to limit the Uyghur population by compelling women to be sterilized or to have intrauterine devices inserted. If a woman refused, the authorities would reputedly send her to the "training camps." Other sources, often via the Uyghur expat communities, have accused officials and guards of torturing or raping detainees, injecting them with unspecified drugs, and sterilizing women. The PRC denies these accusations, but again, without access to the "centers" or "camps," neither the denials nor the accusations can be confirmed.

On the other side, Xi and other leaders have been concerned about the Uyghur diaspora and blamed it for instigating some of the violence and resistance in Xinjiang. They have castigated the Uyghur section of the US' Radio Free Asia for inaccurate reporting and the World Uyghur Congress for encouraging dissidents and "splittists." The PRC has portrayed the director of the Uyghur Service of Radio Free Asia as a staunch conservative and fundamentalist Christian and anti-Communist who seeks the overthrow of the atheistic Chinese government. It has also depicted the East Turkistan National Awakening Movement, which was established in 2004 and was based in Washington, DC, as a subversive organization. PRC leaders have been even more critical of the East Turkistan government in exile, which was established in 2017 and challenged the legitimacy of PRC rule over Xinjiang. Its location in Washington, DC, irritated the PRC leaders and prompted them to accuse the United States of interfering in China's internal affairs. PRC officials have also castigated an anti-Communist German who lives in the United States and writes about alleged forced labor and sterilization of Uyghur women. They have also accused some Western newspapers and magazines of publishing articles based on the accounts of expat Uyghurs or staunch anti-Communists without sufficient fact-checking. They would naturally condemn such depictions.

The PRC has not provided proof for its accusations that such organizations as the East Turkistan National Awakening Movement or the World Uyghur Congress were involved in the violence that has afflicted Xinjiang. In any event, it has retaliated against the expats. It has lobbied governments in Central Asia and Turkey to control Uyghurs in their countries and to prevent calls for Uyghur autonomy. In 2020, it requested that Turkey return some of the Uyghur so-called militants to China. Turkey, which has economic ties with the PRC, faces pressure to do so. Other Muslim countries have not called for new PRC policies toward the Uyghurs, their coreligionists, in part perhaps due to commercial relations with and foreign aid from China.

The PRC leadership seems determined to persist with the camps. The questions that loom over the camps are how effective they have been and will be in convincing the vast majority of Uyghurs and other non-Han of the so-called dangers of separatism and Islamic extremism and for how long the government can maintain such a system. Xi and Chen must believe that this policy has worked because there have been no major violent incidents and only a few minor skirmishes since the establishment of the camps in 2017. But is this a calm before the storm? Only time will tell.

A 2020 *New York Times* article reported that an elderly couple who had apparently been placed in the camps was released within a year.[30] Could this be the harbinger of a more moderate approach? Will PRC and local leaders in Xinjiang now place greater emphasis on economic progress for the region? Some reports suggest that some detainees have been released, but critics assert that they are now coerced into working in factories in Xinjiang or in central China and thus separated from their families and culture in an effort to compel them to assimilate into Han society. There have also been claims that the detainees are not paid or are treated as forced laborers, but such assertions cannot be verified. Yet an article in the *New York Times* notes that the researchers at Horizon Advisory, an agency that provides consultations on international issues, "do not provide direct testimony of forced labor. Instead, they present signs of possible coercion from Chinese language documents and news reports, such as programs that may use high pressure recruitment techniques, indoctrinate workers with patriotic or military education, or restrict their movement."[31] On the other hand, there is other evidence of relaxation of some of the restrictive policies.[32] Recent reports suggest that some of the camps have been turned into detainment facilities for criminals, and they house fewer ordinary citizens whom the government wishes to "reeducate." Will this purported change lead to fewer citizens being sent to these camps?

FAILURES AND SUCCESSES AND THE FUTURE

The PRC naturally emphasizes some successes. The reforms starting after Mao Zedong's death in 1976 lifted hundreds of millions in China out of poverty, and Xinjiang was part of that welcome statistic. Education and health facilities have all improved, yet income disparities between Hans and Uyghurs have persisted. A Uyghur middle class has developed as more economic opportunities have arisen for those with the Chinese language and other employment skills. Like the Han, Uyghurs in Xinjiang have developed their own networks to promote their economic interests, and some have prospered. Nonetheless, employment discrimination against Uyghurs persists.

The government proclaims that women have, in theory, achieved legal equality with men and can make their own decisions about their lives. Again, with limited foreign observations, it is difficult to verify this claim. A *New York Times* article about PRC policies toward the Uyghurs reveals that a young Uyghur woman disobeyed her parents and married a Han man, despite the repeated disapproval of her family. Is this common, or is it unusual? Even with such Communist policies, problems will remain. Some Uyghurs and other non-Han believe that their culture and ethnicity would be subsumed into Han civilization. Critics demand changes in PRC policies related to music, poetry and literature, clothing, and personal styles and adornments, all of which comprise the Uyghur heritage. They also point to the oppressive policies in Xinjiang.

The PRC has attempted to rebut criticism about infringement on non-Han culture by asserting that integration and fusion have been the norm for many societies. Citing the experiences of Russia and the United States, PRC leaders proclaim that they are on solid ground in promoting assimilation, emphasizing the concept of the "melting pot."[33] The question that remains is would the PRC abandon policies that infringe on Uyghur and other non-Han culture and religion? The government has at various times adopted moderate policies concerning Uyghur language, arts, and religion. If PRC leaders truly believed in the Marxist ideology that economic changes, basically the transition to Communism and the rise of the proletariat, would lead to social and economic quality and would inexorably alter the superstructure of religion and culture, why persist in restraining the Uyghurs' expression of their culture?

What are the prospects for the Uyghurs? Xinjiang is landlocked, and the establishment of an independent country may not be the optimal solution. Xinjiang's access to markets would rely heavily on China and Central Asia, and it would lose aid from China. In any event, the independent Central Asian countries do not provide an attractive model. Tajikistan and Kyrgyzstan are among the world's poorest countries; Uzbekistan and Turkmenistan have natural resources, but inequitable distribution of income has translated into high rates of poverty. Kazakhstan is the exception because its oil reserves have lifted its economy. All five countries have authoritarian governments. Most of Xinjiang's population would probably not wish to follow the example of these Central Asian countries.

Other nearby countries could generate more problems for China. Muslim extremists from South and Southeast Asia and the Middle East could prove a threat because their views could filter into Xinjiang, and they could influence and provide training in combat for the Uyghur emigres who seek independence. Uyghur militants have been identified in Indonesia, and some have fought in the Syrian civil war. A few have cooperated with the Taliban in Afghanistan and Pakistan, but it seems likely that they seek the military training and do not share the Taliban's ideology. The PRC has pressured governments in Asia not only to monitor the activities of Uyghur émigrés and their relations with Islamic extremists, but also to ban Uyghur demonstrations in their lands. The United States' withdrawal of its troops from Afghanistan in 2021 poses challenges and opportunities for the PRC. US troops had kept the Taliban and religious extremists at bay from the ninety miles' border between China and Afghanistan. The Taliban's territorial gains since the US withdrawal and the potential for their assisting Uyghur militants concerns the Chinese. PRC officials seek to prevent such a scenario by offering economic incentives, the Belt and Road Initiative, purchase of minerals from Afghanistan, and foreign aid, as part of a package to the Taliban. The Taliban have met with the Chinese. At the same time, PRC officials have been in touch with other Afghans and may be attempting to broker a deal between the Taliban and other Afghan actors. A more stable Afghanistan would be in China's interest. Will a deal emerge by which the Taliban and the Afghan government restrain Uyghur militants in Afghanistan and receive, in return, Chinese economic support?

US POLICY

What is the most productive role for the United States? The United States has been involved in three wars in Asia in the twentieth century, which confirms that it has interests in the Pacific. The initial founding of the PRC in 1949 caused consternation in the US government, leading to a lack of formal relations between the two countries until the 1970s. Mao Zedong's death in 1976 and the ensuing reforms in the PRC relieved some but not all of the tensions. However, Xi Jinping's ascent to power in 2012–2013 led to changes in policy—including replacement and, occasionally, imprisonment of corrupt officials—and a more aggressive policy toward the Uyghurs. Disagreements between China and the United States have accelerated. The United States has accused China of human rights abuses and challenged China's efforts at claiming territory in the South China Seas. Since 2018, the differing objectives of China and the United States have led to conflict over trade and tariffs, theft of intellectual property, spying, cyberattacks, and the statuses of Hong Kong and Taiwan, among other matters. Deterioration in relations even prompted some Americans to promote a boycott of the Walt Disney movie *Mulan* because part of the film was set in Xinjiang, and the producers acknowledged the assistance of Xinjiang government officials.[34] Anti-Chinese attitudes and policies, have intensified in the United States, with Xinjiang as one bone of contention. Tensions have escalated dramatically since 2017, in large part because COVID-19 originated in China, and some in the United States have blamed the Chinese for what they refer to as the "China virus." Unprovoked attacks on Asians in the United States have also contributed to deterioration in relations.

Xinjiang has proved to be a stumbling block in Sino-American relations. A serious American proposal has been to undermine China's global supply chains by emphasizing purchase of US goods produced in the United States. China, with the world's second largest economy, could initiate reprisals. Similarly, calls on US investors to divest from Chinese stocks and to pressure US companies to curtail business with China might not be effective; China could find other investors and other markets.

The United States had been criticizing the PRC's and Xi Jinping's policies in Xinjiang for some time, but it took decisive action in the fall of 2019. The Congress passed the Uyghur Human Rights Policy Act of 2019, which required US government agencies to issue reports on Chinese treatment of Uyghurs, the number of Uyghurs detained in camps, the use of forced labor, the surveillance of Uyghurs, and the protection of Uyghurs living in the United States.[35] At almost the same time, the US Department of State announced visa restrictions on Chinese officials involved in the alleged detention of Uyghurs and banned the export of US goods produced for China's Public Security Bureaus and commercial companies.[36]

Within a few months, the United States banned or imposed sanctions on the Chinese-owned social networking service TikTok, the social messaging service WeChat, and the technology company Huawei. In late July of 2020, the government sanctioned the leaders of the *bingtuan*, who would not be allowed access to property or financial institutions. The PRC retaliated by imposing sanctions on US senators and limiting commercial relations. United Kingdom politicians have joined in this criticism of the PRC's policies in Xinjiang and have proposed a boycott of the 2022 Winter Olympics in Beijing, which has enraged the Chinese leaders. The Canadian government labeled the PRC's policy toward the Uyghurs as genocide, but Canada's historical treatment of its indigenous population weakened its position. From the 1880s to 1990, the government forcibly placed about

150,000 indigenous children in boarding schools, and members of the indigenous community have recently discovered hundreds of unmarked graves of children who died of neglect or disease in such schools.[37]

In the waning days of the Trump administration, the US government took additional steps. It banned the import of tomatoes and cotton from Xinjiang, claiming that they were produced with forced labor, and formally accused the PRC of genocide against Uyghurs.[38] The government demanded that US companies, as well as firms whose countries were allied with the United States, examine their supply chains to root out cotton from Xinjiang. The result was predictable: Chinese consumers, probably egged on by the government, initiated boycotts of companies that followed the instructions from the United States or included criticisms of China's use of forced labor on their Web pages. At least two major companies abandoned their critiques, and several others hedged. On another note, in a book published in 2020, the pope had mentioned the "poor Uyghurs" among the "persecuted" peoples. The PRC stated that his assertions had "no factual basis."[39] The Biden administration has, in general, continued these policies, and the Chinese have responded that the United States is treating China as an "imaginary enemy."[40]

The PRC has actively responded to these laws, accusations, and restrictions. It has accused the United States of interfering in China's internal affairs and of attempting to create disturbances in China. PRC leaders believe that the United States seeks to cause disruptions in Xinjiang because of the area's natural resources and its significance in the Belt and Road Initiative.[41] They have asserted that the present system in Xinjiang is uniquely appropriate for the people and the region. The PRC leaders have also countered that these accusations reflect US hypocrisy. They have pointed to the US mistreatment of Native Americans and African

Americans, citing them as examples of the government's policies toward minorities and as human rights violations and have mentioned the disparities in education, employment, income, and life spans between Caucasians and African Americans. Several PRC officials have stated that the United States, considering its treatment of minorities, is in no position to lecture other countries on human rights and democracy. They have even alluded to the Holocaust in rebutting criticism from the European countries. The United States is in a weak position in such a debate. Punitive reprimands will most likely elicit responses about US misdeeds. This policy does not seem effective.

A belligerent policy concerning treatment of Uyghurs may not produce the desired result and may instead generate blowback from the PRC. So far, it has elicited a PRC response that the United States is interfering in China's internal affairs. US sanctions have been met with PRC sanctions. It is important to note that human rights issues can cut both ways. The PRC has and will accuse the United States of violations in treatment of African Americans, Native Americans, and refugees. This is not to say that the United States should abandon all critiques of the PRC's policies in Xinjiang. The United States can weigh in on the PRC's overly liberal use of capital punishment, possible exploitation of non-Han workers, and, if strong evidence exists, forced sterilizations or torture in Xinjiang.

J. Stapleton Roy, a former US ambassador to China, has also questioned the United States' policy toward Xinjiang. In a recent interview, he said, "Is our purpose to remake other countries in our image? . . . When people say we should be forcing the Chinese to deal better with the Uyghurs . . . what should the Chinese be doing to force us to address our own racial problems better? . . . Most Americans would say that's a silly question because it's clearly not within the capability of China to know how to run the

U.S. . . . It is presumptuous of us to think that we have the tools to force China to do things that are embedded at the heart of its own problems of domestic governance." He adds that the embargo on Xinjiang cotton "may make us feel virtuous, but in terms of affecting the outcome in China, I would say it's not effective."[42]

Professor Pei Mingxin of Claremont McKenna College has proposed an interesting plan to deal with the internment or reeducation camps, which, he believes, have created a public relations disaster for China. He assumes that the ideological indoctrination in the camps will be ineffective and suggests that the camps be disbanded and that the government grant $14,000 to each detainee, a grand total of $14 billion, if a million inhabitants are truly in the camps. He also advises the PRC to make microfinancing available for Uyghur startups, to share revenues from Xinjiang's natural resources with the Uyghurs, to recruit more Uyghurs into the government, to limit Han in-migration into Xinjiang, and to end unnecessary attacks on Islam.[43] The PRC has already implemented some of these economic policies to prevent violence and to win over the Uyghurs. Would Professor Pei's more inclusive proposals generate less violence and better relations in Xinjiang?

Another possibility that could be explored is a division into a North Xinjiang, where the Han would be in the majority, and a South Xinjiang, with a largely non-Han population. Within North Xinjiang, Turfan, in which Uyghurs comprise 70 percent of the population; the Altay region, where Kazakhs constitute 51 percent of the population; and the Mongolian areas of Bayangolin and Bortala would form autonomous prefectures. Interestingly enough, Guo Rongxing, a professor at Beijing University, broached this proposal.[44] Would non-Han accept this organization if they had guarantees for the preservation of their culture and heritage and equitable economic opportunities? Would the PRC accept limitations on its powers in the non-Han regions? Would this be a utopian plan, with limited prospects for implementation and success, or could it limit the disturbances that have afflicted Xinjiang?

Some observers have speculated about a collapse of the PRC similar to the fall of the USSR. Yet there are differences between the two Communist countries. The USSR faced economic stagnation, unsustainable military spending, and the discontent of the population, as well as a questioning of Communist ideology, via glasnost, or more open government; and perestroika, or restructuring of the economy. China has had four decades of a relatively robust economy and has, thus far, been able to cover increased military expenditures. Mikhail Gorbachev, general secretary of the Communist Party of the USSR, sought to liberalize the government and economy, which led to dramatic changes, whereas Xi Jinping has attempted to consolidate power within the existing, if somewhat altered, Communist system. Dissatisfaction with the USSR was pervasive; no persuasive evidence indicates that China faces similar discontent. A complete economic collapse of the PRC might give rise to such disarray, an eventuality that could generate calls for changes in any state. The PRC economy seems stable, albeit without the dramatic growth of the late twentieth century.

In the remote possibility of such a collapse, what would be the prospects for Xinjiang? Would the Uyghurs achieve the unity that has thus far proved elusive? Or would they, as some observers have speculated, identify with specific oases, with one or two oases serving as sites for a federation? Would Islam offer a unifying force and bring together the Uyghurs, Kazakhs, Kyrgyz, and perhaps even the Hui, or ethnic Chinese Muslims, in Xinjiang? Would such an alignment allow for closer economic relations with Central Asia, Russia, and even Turkey? All of this speculation would still imply that Xinjiang would remain part of China but with greater flexibility and autonomy.

The view I presented forty-five years ago still reflects the current situation: "Minority problems in most societies have proven enormously resistant to easy or rapid solutions . . . It is not yet clear that the People's Republic of China constitutes an exception."

NOTES

1. J. Todd Reed and Diana Raschke, *The ETIM: China's Militants and the Global Terrorist Threat* (Santa Barbara, CA: Greenwood, 2010), 35–41.

2. Reed and Raschke, *The ETIM*, 1. The authors also stated, "The Eastern Turkistan terrorists are clearly connected with international terrorist forces," 129.

3. Joanne Smith Finley, "'Ethnic Anomaly' or Modern Uyghur Survivor? A Case Study of the *Minkaohan* Hybrid Identity in Xinjiang," in Ildikó Bellér-Hann, M. Cristina Cesàro, Rachel Harris, and Joanne Smith Finley, *Situating the Uighurs Between China and Central Asia* (Hampshire, UK: Ashgate, 2007), 219–38.

4. See Yangbin Chen, *Muslim Uyghur Students in a Chinese Boarding School* (Lanham, MD: Lexington, 2008) for this study.

5. Timothy Grose, *Negotiating Inseparability in China: The Xinjiang Class and the Dynamics of Uyghur Identity* (Hong Kong: Hong Kong University Press, 2019).

6. Grose, *Negotiating Inseparability in China*, 20.

7. On the higher standard of living of such educated Uyghurs and their ability to purchase expensive apartments, see Grose, *Negotiating Inseparability in China*, 95 and 104; on limited opportunities for employment, 108.

8. Joanne Smith Finley, *The Art of Symbolic Resistance: Uyghur Identities and Uyghur-Han Relations in Contemporary Xinjiang* (Leiden: Brill, 2013), 298.

9. Amelia Pang, "Tied to a Genocide in China," *New York Times*, January 17, 2021, 10, disapproved, noting that such encouragement would ultimately lead to an erosion of Uyghur culture. Uyghur parents appear, in some cases, to have disapproved of intermarriage even of Uyghur men and Han women. See Grose, *Negotiating Inseparability in China*, 60–61. In addition, parents sometimes pressured educated Uyghur women to marry at a young age. See Grose, *Negotiating Inseparability in China*, 93–97.

10. Joanne Smith Finley, "Contesting Harmony through TV Drama: Ethnic Intermarriage in *Xinjiang Girls*," in Trine Brox and Ildikó Bellér-Hann, eds., *On the Fringes of the Harmonious Society* (Copenhagen: NIAS Press, 2014), 278, 276.

11. See A. S. Bhalla and Shufang Qiu, *Poverty and Inequality among Chinese Minorities* (London: Routledge, 2006).

12. James Millward, *Violent Separatism in Xinjiang: A Critical Assessment* (Washington, DC: East-West Center, 2004), 32.

13. James Millward described these attitudes in *Eurasian Crossroads: A History of Xinjiang* (New York: Columbia University Press, 2007), 340–41.

14. On the TIP, see Sean Roberts, *The War on the Uyghurs: China's Internal Campaign against a Muslim Minority* (Princeton, NJ: Princeton University Press, 2020), 86–95, who also writes that the TIP leaders "were fully aligned with Al-Qaeda in northern Waziristan" (119). The TIP's videos "were obvious attempts to inspire the Uyghurs inside China to wage jihad against the state," and its leaders sought to get internationalist jihadist networks to turn their attention toward China as an enemy and potential target.

15. Sean Roberts writes that the "violence was a spontaneous response to security forces' aggressive attempts to stop the marchers from advancing" (Roberts, *War on the Uyghurs*, 146), which places the blame on the Han for this violence. As he then notes, "Uyghurs throughout the city set vehicles on fire, destroyed stores, and began attacking Han civilians, leaving a reported 156 dead" (146). He acknowledges that 156 Han were killed. Raffi Khatchadourian, "Ghost Walls," *New Yorker*,

April 12, 2021, 30, writes misleadingly about the Urumchi riots: "The police cracked down, and riots erupted. Hundreds of people were injured or killed, and hundreds were arrested. More than forty Uyghurs were presumed disappeared." He fails to mention that the vast majority of the dead were Han.

16. Rongxing Guo, ed., *Multicultural China: A Statistical Yearbook (2014)* (Berlin: Springer, 2015), 222–27.

17. See A. Doak Barnett, *China on the Eve of Communist Takeover* (New York: Praeger, 1963), 238–81, for his report.

18. Xi has had at least two formative experiences relating to the United States. First, during his rise to power, he spent two weeks studying agricultural technology in Iowa, a state he revisited as head of state. Second, his daughter received her undergraduate degree at Harvard University.

19. Rongxing Guo, *China's Spatial (Dis)integration: Political Economy of the Interethnic Unrest in Xinjiang* (Waltham, MA: Chandos, 2015), 63.

20. Darren Byler, *Chinese Infrastructures of Population Management on the New Silk Road* (Washington, DC: Woodrow Wilson Center, 2020), 24, writes, "The population of low-level police assistants and neighborhood watch unit personnel in Xinjiang is without parallel in the rest of the country." This is no doubt true, but no other section of the country had experienced the same violence.

21. Byler, *Chinese Infrastructures of Population Management*, 25, asserts that religious practice "is now only the domain of a very small number of elderly protected individuals."

22. Matt Rivers, "More than 100 Uyghur Graveyards Demolished by Chinese Authorities, Satellite Images Show," CNN, January 2, 2020.

23. Liu Xin and Fan Lingzhi, "Xinjiang Residents Debunk CNN Report of Cemetery Destruction," *Global Times*, January 6, 2020.

24. See preface, note 7, for more information about this individual and his views.

25. Sarah A. Topol, "The Disappeared," *New York Times Magazine*, February 2, 2020, 43.

26. "World Bank Statement on Review of Project in Xinjiang," www.worldbank.org.news.statement, November 11, 2019.

27. *Global Times*, November 27, 2020.

28. Roberts, *War on the Uyghurs*, 242.

29. Zachary Evans, "Former US Ambassador to China Claims Hong Kong Protesters "Went Too Far,' Denies China Carrying Out Genocide of Uyghurs," *National Review*, September 17, 2020. Mr. Roy's brother David Todd Roy was professor of Chinese literature at the University of Chicago and translated *Jin ping mei*, one of China's greatest novels.

30. Topol, "The Disappeared," 44–45.

31. Ana Swanson and Christopher Buckley, "Chinese and Solar Companies Tied to Use of Forced Labor," *New York Times*, January 9, 2021, A9.

32. Roberts, *War on the Uyghurs*, 238.

33. Sean Roberts writes that "such violent attempts to destroy and forcibly assimilate ethnic or national groups are generally no longer acceptable to the international community" and asserts that the PRC promotes "coerced miscegenation" in his book (200, 213). It is true that the PRC offers rewards for Han and Uyghur intermarriages, but claims of forced intermarriages would need stronger evidence.

34. Amy Qin and Edward Wong, "Calls Grow to Boycott 'Mulan' over China's Treatment of Uyghur Muslims," *New York Times*, September 92, 2020, A10.

35. "Uighur Human Rights Policy Act of 2019," https://gop-foreignaffairs.house.gov>legislation>h-r-64 (accessed January 31, 2020).

36. "US Department of State Imposes Visa Restrictions on Chinese Officials for Repression in Xinjiang," www.state.gov>u-s-department-of-state-imposes-restrictions-on-Chinese-officials-for-repression-in-Xinjiang (accessed December 15, 2019).

37. Ian Austen, "Discovery of Graves Bolsters Indigenous Push for Reckoning in Canada," *New York Times*, June 27, 6.

38. "Forced Labor in Cotton Fields," *Wall Street Journal*, December 15, 2020; Ana Swanson, "US Bans Cotton and Tomatoes from Chinese Region," *New York Times*, January 14, 2021, B4; Amy Qin, "Trump's Last-Minute Moves against China Complicate Biden's Agenda," *New York Times*, January 21, 2021, A10; Edward Wong and Chris Buckley,

"U.S. State Dept. Accuses China of Uighur Genocide," *New York Times*, January 20, 2021, A9.

39. Gaia Pianigiani, "Pope Calls Uyghurs 'Persecuted,' Arousing Fury in Beijing," *New York Times*, November 25, 2020, A12.

40. See, for example, Steven Lee Myers and Amy Qin, "Biden Has Angered Beijing, but the Communist Party Is Pushing Back," *New York Times*, July 21, 2021, A10.

41. See Tom O'Connor, "China Says US 'Ulterior Motive' in Xinjiang Genocide Claim Is Inciting Unrest," https://www.newsweek.com/china-says-us-ulterior-motive-xinjiang-genocide-cliam-inciting-unrest-1589334, May 6, 2021.

42. David Barboza, "Stapleton Roy Asks What the U.S Wants from the China Relationship," https://www.thewirechina.com, July 25, 2021.

43. https.//asia.nikkei.com/opinion/China-needs-an-exit-strategy-from-xinjiang2, August 8, 2020.

44. Guo, *China's Spatial (Dis)integration*, 149–55.

BIBLIOGRAPHY

I refer the reader to books on Xinjiang, but not articles, which may be difficult to access. The works on the post-1949 period represent a diversity of views, not just my own. I regret that articles by such individuals as James Leibold, Rémi Castets, and others who have different viewpoints are not included.

GENERAL WORKS

Millward, James. *Eurasian Crossroads: A History of Xinjiang*. New York: Columbia University Press, 2007.

Rossabi, Morris. *China and Inner Asia from 1368 to the Present Day*. London: Thames and Hudson, 1975.

HISTORY TO 1949

Barber, Elizabeth. *The Mummies of Urumchi*. New York: Norton, 1999.

Barnett, A. Doak. *China on the Eve of Communist Takeover*. New York: Praeger, 1963.

Benson, Linda. *The Ili Rebellion: The Moslem Challenge to Chinese Authority in Xinjiang, 1944–1949*. Armonk, NY: Sharpe, 1990.

Brophy, David. *Uyghur Nation: Reform and Revolution on the Russia-China Frontier*. Cambridge, MA: Harvard University Press, 2016.

Danielson, Sarah. *The Explorer's Roundup to National Socialism: Sven Hedin, Geography, and the Path to Genocide.* Farnham, UK: Ashgate, 2012.

Forbes, Andrew. *Warlords and Muslims in Chinese Central Asia: A Political History of Republican Xinjiang.* Cambridge: Cambridge University Press, 1986.

Golden, Peter. *Central Asia in World History.* Oxford: Oxford University Press, 2011.

Hansen, Valerie. *The Silk Road: A New History.* New York: Oxford University Press, 2012.

Hopkirk, Peter. *Foreign Devils on the Silk Road.* London: John Murray, 1980.

Kim, Hodong. *Holy War in China: The Muslim Rebellion and State in Chinese Central Asia, 1864–1877.* Stanford, CA: Stanford University Press, 2004.

Kim, Kwangmin. *Borderland Capitalism.* Stanford, CA: Stanford University Press, 2016.

Klimeš, Ondřej. *Struggle by the Pen: The Uyghur Discourse of National and National Interest, 1900–1949.* Leiden: Brill, 2005.

Manz, Beatrice. *The Rise and Rule of Tamerlane.* Cambridge, MA: Cambridge University Press, 1999.

Perdue, Peter. *China Marches West: The Qing Conquest of Central Eurasia.* Cambridge, MA: Harvard University Press, 2005.

Rossabi, Morris. *Khubilai Khan: His Life and Times.* Berkeley: University of California Press, 1988.

Tucker, Robert. *Stalin as Revolutionary, 1879–1929.* New York: Norton, 1973.

Whiting, Allen, and Sheng Shih-ts'ai. *Sinkiang: Pawn or Pivot?* East Lansing: Michigan State University Press, 1958.

COMMUNIST ERA

Barnett, A. Doak. *China's Far West: Four Decades of Change.* Boulder, CO: Westview, 1993.

Bellér-Hann, Ildikó, M. Cristina Cesàro, Rachel Harris, and Joanne Smith Finley. *Situating the Uyghurs Between China and Central Asia*. Hampshire, UK: Ashgate, 2007.

Benson, Linda, and Ingyar Svanberg. *China's Last Nomads: The History and Culture of the Kazaks*. Armonk: Sharpe, 1998.

Bhalla, A. S., and Shufang Qiu. *Poverty and Inequality among Chinese Minorities*. New York: Routledge, 2006.

Bovingdon, Gardner. *Autonomy in Xinjiang: Han Nationalist Imperatives and Uyghur Discontent*. Washington, DC: East-West Center, 2004.

———. *The Uyghurs: Strangers in Their Own Land*. New York: Columbia University Press, 2010.

Brox, Trine, and Ildikó Bellér-Hann, eds. *On the Fringes of the Harmonious Society: Tibetans and Uyghurs in Socialist China*. Copenhagen: NIAS, 2014.

Byler, Darren. *Chinese Infrastructures of Population Management on the New Silk Road*. Washington, DC: Woodrow Wilson Center, 2020.

Chen, Yangbin. *Muslim Uyghur Students in a Chinese Boarding School*. Lanham, MD: Lexington, 2008.

Clarke, Michael. *Xinjiang and China's Rise in Central Asia*. London: Routledge, 2011.

Cliff, Tom. *Oil and Water: Being Han in Xinjiang*. Chicago: University of Chicago Press, 2016.

Dautcher, Jay. *Down a Narrow Road: Identity and Masculinity in a Uyghur Community in Xinjiang*. Cambridge, MA: Harvard University Press, 2009.

De Jong, Frederick. *Uyghur Texts in Context*. Leiden: Brill, 2018.

Dreyer, June Teufel. *China's Forty Millions*. Cambridge, MA: Harvard University Press, 1976,

Dwyer, Arienne. *The Xinjiang Conflict: Uyghur Identity, Language Policy, and Political Discourse*. Washington, DC: East-West Center, 2005.

Finley, Joanne Smith. *The Art of Symbolic Resistance: Uyghur Identities and Uyghur-Han Relations in Contemporary Xinjiang*. Leiden: Brill, 2013.

Gladney, Dru. *Muslim China: Ethnic Nationalism in the People's Republic*. Cambridge, MA: Harvard University Press, 1991.

Grose, Timothy. *Negotiating Inseparability in China: The Xinjiang Class and the Dynamics of Uyghur Identity*. Hong Kong: Hong Kong University Press, 2019.

Guo, Rongxing. *China's Spatial (Dis)integration: Political Economy of the Interethnic Unrest in Xinjiang*. Waltham, MA: Chandos, 2015.

———. *Multicultural China: A Statistical Yearbook (2014)*. Heidelberg: Springer, 2015.

Hillman, Ben, and Gray Tuttle, eds. *Ethnic Conflict and Protest in Tibet and in Xinjiang*. New York: Columbia University Press, 2016.

Holdstock, Nick. *China's Forgotten People: Xinjiang, Terror, and the Chinese State*. London: Tauris, 2015.

Hua, Shiping, ed. *Islam and Democratization in Asia*. Amherst, NY: Cambria Press, 2009.

Jacobs, Justin. *Xinjiang and the Modern Chinese State*. Seattle: University of Washington Press, 2016.

Kadeer, Rebiya. *Dragon Fighter: One Woman's Struggle for Peace with China*. Carlsbad, CA: Kales Press, 2011.

Millward, James. *Violent Separatism in Xinjiang: A Critical Assessment*. Washington, DC: East-West Center, 2003.

Reed, J. Todd, and Diana Raschke. *The ETIM: China's Militants and the Global Terrorist Threat*. Santa Barbara, CA: Greenwood, 2010.

Roberts, Sean. *The War on the Uyghurs: China's Internal Campaign against a Muslim Minority*. Princeton, NJ: Princeton University Press, 2020.

Rossabi, Morris, ed. *Governing China's Multiethnic Frontiers*. Seattle: University of Washington Press, 2004.

Rudelson, Justin. *Oasis Identities: Uyghur Nationalism along China's Silk Road*. New York: Columbia University Press, 1997.

Scalapino, Robert, ed. *Elites in the People's Republic of China*. Seattle: University of Washington Press, 1972.

Starr, S. Frederick, ed. *The New Silk Roads. Transport and Trade in Greater Central Asia*. Washington, DC: School of Advanced International Studies, 2007.

———. *Xinjiang: China's Muslim Borderland*. Armonk, NY: Sharpe, 2004.

Thum, Rian. *The Sacred Routes of Uyghur History*. Cambridge, MA: Harvard University Press, 2014.

Zhang, Xiaowei. *Ethnicity in China*. Cambridge, MA: Polity Press, 2015.

———. *Uyghur Concept of Family and Society*. New York: Routledge, 2019.

INDEX

Afghanistan, 71, 77, 83, 94, 97, 122–123; Islamic fundamentalists and, 86–87, 138
Aksu, 37, 71, 114
Altai Mountains, 2
Altay, 32–33, 143
Altishahr, 37
Amu Dar'ya River, 4

Bachu, 114
Baicheng killings, 124
Baikal, Lake, 36
Bandung Conference, 46
Baren incident, 76–79, 85
Barnett, A. Doak, 39–40, 43, 69, 106
begs, 14–15, 70
Beijing, ix, 36, 72, 74–75, 113; bombings in, 86
Beijing Normal University, 75
Beijing time, 78–79
Belt and Road Initiative, viii, 118–19, 138; environmental problems and, 119; loans and, 119; unstable lands and, 119
Beshbaliq, 9
Black Sea, 4
boarding schools and colleges, 95–96
Bolshevik Revolution, 23

Bortala, 143
Boxer rebellion, 20
British Museum, 22
Buddhism, 5, 8
Buffett, Warren, 88
Burhan Shahidi, 34–35, 44
Bush, George W., 89

Canada critique, 140–41
Caspian Sea, 4
cemeteries, 107
Central Asia, 78–79; borders with China, 84; Chinese trade with, 92, 97, 116–17; fundamentalists in, 86 ; threats from, 77–78, 83, 92, 117
Central Asia Belt, 118
Central Nationalities Institute, 74
Chaghadai, 10–11
Changan (Xi'an), 8
Chen Quanguo, 124–28, 131, 135; convenience police stations and, 124–25
Chiang Kai-shek, 23–24, 29–30, 32–35, 41; Sheng Shicai and, 32
China Infrastructure Investment Bank, 118
China National Petroleum Company, 108, 117

China Pakistan Economic Corridor, 118
Chinese Islamic Association, 44–45
Chinese People's Consultative Conference, 88
Chinggis Khan, 9–10
Commission for the Study of the Tribal Composition of the Population of Russia, 28–29
Common Program, 42
communes, 52–53, 55, 58
convenience police stations, 124–25
Coq, Albert von le, 22
cotton, 3, 58, 67, 70, 74, 80, 87, 106, 117; boycott of, 130, 141, 143; depletion of water and, 3, 62; pesticides and, 62, 70, 74
Counterterrorism Law, 122
cyberattacks, 139–40

Daidu (Beijing), 10
Dalai Lama, 13, 57
Deng Xiaoping, 59, 61–62
doppas, 107
drug addiction, 97
Dunhuang, 8, 22

East Turkistan, 5
East Turkistan National Awakening Movement, 134
East Turkistan Islamic Movement (ETIM), 93–94, 102
Eastern Mongols, 1
Eastern Turkistan government in exile, 134
Eastern Turkistan Islamic Party, 77
Eastern Turkistan Islamic Republic, 29–30
Eastern Turkistan Republic [second], 32–33; airplane crash and, 36–37, 43; USSR and, 34–36

Erawan (Bangkok) shrine attacks, 120, 122–23
Ethnological Museum (Berlin), 22
Eurasian Land Belt, 118
expatriates, ix–x, 77, 133, 135

Feng Yuxiang ("Christian General"), 25
forced labor accusations, 128–30, 135–36
Four Modernizations, 65

Galdan, 12–13
Gang of Four, 61, 65
Gaspirali, Ismail, 28
Gates, Bill, 88
Gauthier, Ursula, 124
"genocide" accusations, 141
Ghulja, 34
Gorbachev, Mikhail, 144
Great Firewall, 120
Great Game, 18
Great Leap Forward, 52, 68–69, 132; failures of, 53, 57, 61; Islam and, 54–55
Great Proletarian Cultural Revolution, 59–61, 65–66, 69, 73, 94, 115, 132
Great Wall of Steel, 120
Gromyko, Andrei, 52
Grose, Timothy, 96–97
guanxi, 98
Guo Rongxing and division of Xinjiang, 143
Guomindang, 29, 32–35, 51

Hajj, 44, 58, 61, 68
Hami, 2, 4, 5, 12–13;
Han (ethnic Chinese), vii, 44–45, 47; arrival in Xinjiang and, 19–20; lack of migration and, 5, 7–8 ;

migration to Xinjiang and, 48, 50, 59, 66, 71, 74–75, 79–81, 99, 117; Uyghur stereotypes of, 46
Han chauvinism, 66
Hangzhou, 113
Haussmann, Georges-Eugène, 113
Hedin, Sven, 21–22
hexie shehui (*harmonious society*), 110
HIV-AIDS, 97
Hong Kong, 139–40
Horizon Advisory, 135–36
household registration (*hukou*), 81
Hu Yaobang, 66, 72, 75
Huawei, 140
Hui (Dungans, Chinese Muslims), vii, 16, 30–31, 39, 47
Human Rights Watch Asia, 130
Hundred Flowers, 49–50
hutong, 113

Id Kah mosque, 38, 112, 119
Indonesia, 118, 138
Inner Mongolia, 1, 126
Inner Mongolian Autonomous Region, 99
Institute for the Study of Islamic Texts, 79
Iraq, 94
Isa Yusuf Alptekin, 41
Islam, 5, 14–15, 19–20; arrival of, 8–9; attacks on, 61, 126; beards and, 91, 107, 126 ; cemeteries and, 107; fundamentalists and, 83, 86, 138; limitations on, 45, 54–55, 77–79, 82, 87, 94–95, 98–100, 107; moderate policy toward, 65, 67; veils and, 91, 126
Islamic Movement of Uzbekistan, 84
ISIS, 122

Jadidism, 21, 28
Jiang Qing, 61, 65
Jiang Zemin, 81
Jin Shuren, 25, 30

Kadeer, Rebiya, 88–89, 105; arrest of, 89 ; documentary about, 113
Karakoram, 87
Karame oil fields, 117
karez, 2–3
Karimov, Islam, 84, 92
Kashgar, viii, 4, 18, 21, 29–30, 37–38, 67–68, 71, 76–77, 85, 100; attack on police, 103 ; razing of old town, 111–13; violence in, 124
Kashgaria, 22
Kazakhs, vii, 31–34, 38–39, 47, 51, 78, 85, 99–100, 143; migration of, 55–56
Kazakhstan, 3, 18, 31, 78–79, 83, 92, 116, 118, 137
Khaidu, 10
Khara Khoto, 22
Khojas, 15
Khoqand, 15–16, 18
Khorgos, 116
Khotan, 2, 4, 8, 22, 37–38, 85; attack on police and, 114 ; cemetery and, 126–27
Khrushchev, Nikita, 49, 51–52
Khubilai Khan, 10
Kizil caves, 22
Kunlun, 2
Koran, 62, 68, 79
Korla, 4, 117
Kozlov, Pyotr Kuzmich, 22
Kōzui Ōtani, 22
Kucha, 22, 103
Kunming attack, 120

Kyrgyz, vii, 9, 34, 39, 47; assassination of Chinese ambassador in, 85
Kyrgyzstan, 31, 92, 94, 116

Law on Regional Autonomy for Minority Nationalities, 72
Li Hongzhi, 17
Liu Shaoqi, 58–59
Lop Nor, 62, 71, 74

Ma Zhongying, 30–31
mahtabs, 38
Manicheism, 8–9
Mao Zedong, 31–32, 36, 116; death of, 61, 88; Great Proletarian Cultural Revolution and, 59–60; Hundred Flowers and, 49–50; minorities and, 42–43; swim in Yangtze and, 59; Tibet and, 57; USSR and, 41–42, 49, 52
mäshräp (gatherings), 20, 38, 85, 97
Matsu, 52
mazars (shrines), 20, 54, 126–27
Millward, James, 102
minkaohan, 95, 98
minkaomin, 94
Mongolian People's Republic, 55, 57
Mongols, vii
Museé Guimet, 22
Muslim countries and China, 39, 46
mummies, 6

Nanjing, 24, 30, 34
Nasser, Gamal Abdel, 46
National Endowment for Democracy, 89
National [Chinese] People's Consultative Conference, 36–37, 42

negdel, 55
Nerchinsk, Treaty of 1689, 13
Nestorian Christianity, 5, 8
New Han, 108, 118
Nian rebellion, 20
Nixon, Richard, 61
Niyazov, Saparmyrat, 92
North Atlantic Treaty Organization (NATO), 92
nuclear testing, 82, 87

Old Han, 108, 118
Olympics (2008), 103
One Thousand Mothers' Movement, 88
Opium War (1839–1842), 17, 20
Osman Batur, 33, 43
Ottoman Turks, 21

Paired Assistance Program (*duikuo zhiyuan*), 97, 110–11
Pakistan, 71, 83, 97; Islamic fundamentalists in, 86–87, 102, 114, 122–23, 138
Pamirs, 2
Panthay rebellion, 20
Paris, 113
Pei Mingxin, 143
Pelliot, Paul, 22
Pentagon, 93
People's Liberation Army (PLA), 35, 72
Production and Construction Corps (*bingtuan*), 43–44, 47, 107–08, 111, 117–18; abolition of, 66; Cultural Revolution and, 60; restoration of 70–71, 74–75, 79, 82; US sanctions against, 140
Public Security Bureau, 140

Qadis, 45
al-Qaeda, 92–94, 102, 122
Qarakhanids, 9
Qocho, 9
Quemoy, 52

Radio Free Asia, 88, 123, 134
Rahile Dawut, 125–26
Ramadan, 100
Raquette, Gustav, 2
Raschke, Diana, 93
Rebiya Kadeer, 88–89, 105; arrest of, 89; documentary about, 113
Rectification campaign, 49–50
Red Army, 23
Red Guards, 59–61, 66
"Red Terror," 46
Reed, J. Todd, 93
rencai (technical experts), 110
"Rhubarb Road," 4
Roy, J. Stapleton, 133, 142–43
Russia, expansion of, 1–2
Russian Orthodox Church, 18

Saifudin Azizi, 37, 42, 44, 48, 48, 50, 60
St. Petersburg, Treaty of (1881), 18, 21, 23
Sabri Masūd, 34
Shah Nameh, 38
Shāhrukh, 9, 12
Shandong, 97
Shanghai Cooperation Organization (SCO), 92
Shaoguan killings, 104, 110
shaoshu minzu, 42
Shenzhen, 111
shequ (neighborhood watch units), 122

Sheng Shicai, 30, 41; relations with USSR, 30–32; Chiang Kai-shek and, 32
Shibo, 39, 47
Siberia, 12
Sidiq Rouzi, 88
Silk Roads, vii–viii, 4–8, 11, 118; Swedes and, 21–22; Tang dynasty and, 8
Smith, Joanne Finley, 95, 98
Sogdians, 8
South China Seas, 139–40
Soviet Union, 30–32, 38–39, 43–44, 47, 50–52, 56, 60, 66; peace with China and, 71; troops in Mongolia and, 72
"splittists," ix, 76, 83, 86, 100, 122, 133–34
Stalin, Joseph, 29–30, 32, 36, 42, 49, 51, 57
Starr, S. Frederick, 100
Stein, Aurel, 22
"Strike Hard" campaign, 86–88, 91, 94, 111
Sufism, 13, 20
Sukarno, 46
surveillance and police, 121–23
Swedish Mission Society, 21
syringe attacks, 105, 112

Tacheng, 32–33
Tahir, Jüme, 119
Taiping Rebellion (1850–1864), 18, 20
Taiwan, 52, 139–40
Tajikistan, 92
Tajiks, 39
Taklamakan desert, 2, 5, 7, 22, 35
talaq, 98–99
Taliban threat, 87, 94, 102, 138

Tamerlane (Temür), 11–12
Tao Zhiyue, 35
Taranchis, 18, 23–24
Tarim River, 3, 5
Thailand, ix
Third World, 46
Three Districts Revolt, 32–33
Three Effendis, 33–34
Three Evils (terrorism, separatism, and religious extremism), 91, 93, 101, 113, 120, 135
Tiananmen attack, 115
Tiananmen killings, 74–75
Tianshan, 2, 5, 71
Tarim Oil Company, 117–18
Tibet, 1, 13, 66, 125–26; rebellion in, 56–57
TikTok, 140
Tohti, Enver, 82
Tohti, Ilham, 123–24
tomato boycott, 141
tribute system, 2, 12
tuntian, 7
Turfan, viii, 2, 4, 12–13, 37, 143; Flaming Cliffs of, 22
Turkestan, 31, 92
Turkey, 135
Turkistan Islamic Party, 102–03
Turkmenistan, 78–79, 83

Uch-Turfan, 37
Uighur Online web site, 123
"Unite as One Family," 122
United States, 139–42; Chinese criticism of, 141–42; ETIM and, 93; expansion of, 1–2; human rights and, 139; trade and tariffs, 139; relations with China, 139–40
Urumchi, viii, 54, 71; bombings in, 86; suspension of Internet in, 105, 109, 112; violence in, 102–06, 109–110, 112, 123 ; railway and, 58; syringe attacks in, 105, 112
Uyghur American Congress, 89
Uyghur Empire (744–840), 5, 8–9
Uyghur East Turkistan Education and Solidarity Association, 119
Uyghur Human Rights Policy Act of 2019, 140
Uyghur script, 10
Uyghurs, 25; affirmative action and, 75, 80; Arabic script and, 56, 68; cadres and, 67, 80–81, 97, 106, 114 ; Chinese language and, 67, 81–82, 114, 126, 95, 132, 136; Cyrillic alphabet and, 56, 62, 68; employment of, 67, 75, 80–81, 96–97, 99, 103–04, 107, 110, 128; higher literacy rate and, 69 ; identity of, 27–31, 38–39, 73, 95–97, 112–13, 137; independence and, 137; intermarriage and, 43, 45, 60, 73–74, 80, 98–99,113; Latin alphabet and, 56, 62; life spans and, 101 ; low wages and, 75, 81–82, 99, 103, 109, 123, 132, 136; limitations on culture and, 68, 78, 100, 107, 109, 113, 120–21, 126, 137 ; literature of, 28; middle class and, 97–98, 101, 136; one child per family and, 68, 76–77, 114; Russian influence on, 27; stereotypes of, 46, 62, 82, 96, 101–02, 107–08; study abroad and, 127; surveillance of, 113, 121–22
Uzbekistan, 18, 31, 94

Vietnam War, 60, 71
Vladivostok, 12

"vocational training centers," 128–36; involuntary nature of, 128, 140; rape accusations in, 133–34; sterilization accusations in, 133–34; torture accusations in, 133–34
Voice of America, 88

Wang Enmao, 48, 60
Wang Lequan, 105, 111–12
Wang Zhen, 36, 43, 48
waqfs, 45–46, 54
Waziristan, 102, 114
WeChat, 140
White Russians, 23
Winter Olympics (2022), 140
women, 43, 45, 68, 73–74, 76–77, 80, 91, 98–99, 106–07, 113, 126
World Trade Center, 93
World Uyghur Congress, 89, 119, 134
Wu, Emperor of Han dynasty, 6–7
Wu Zhongxin, 32
Wu'erkaixi, 75

Xi Jinping, 115, 144; Belt and Road Initiative and, 118–19; Great Proletarian Cultural Revolution and, 115; policies of, 115–17; "vocational training centers" and, 131, 135
xiafang, 53–54
Xiongnu, 6–7
Xinjiang, province of, 18
Xinjiang: China's Muslim Borderland, 100–01
Xinjiang Islamic Association, 68
Xinjiang Technical and Vocational Training Project, 130

Xinjiang University, 48, 69, 106, 114, 126
Xinjiang Uyghur Autonomous Region (XUAR), vii, 47; barefoot doctors in, 69 ; economic growth and, 67, 91, 106, 110, 125, 136 ; education in, 48, 52, 56, 68–69, 95–96; environmental problems and, 62, 67, 87, 99, 117; geography of, 2–3; Great Proletarian Cultural Revolution and, 60; medicine in, 48, 50, 69–70, 101, 106; mineral and natural resources of, 62, 117; nuclear tests and waste and, 62, 101; police in, 125
Xinjiang Work Forum, 110–11

Yang Zengxin, 23; assassination of, 25; relations with USSR, 24; rule of, 23–25
Yantaq, 130
Ya'qub Beg, 16–17
Yarkand, 2, 4, 21, 37, 71; violence in, 124
Yasin, Nurmemet, 100
Yecheng violence, 114
Yengisar (Yangi Hissar), 21, 37
yibu dakaifu, 81
Yili, 32–33, 38, 80; Russians and, 16, 18
Yili River, 3
Yining, 38, 85–86, 99
Yolbars Khan, 41
Young Turks, 27
Yuan Shikai, 23
Yunnan, ix

Zeng Jize, 18
Zhang Chunxian, 111–12

Zhang Qian, 7
Zhang Zhizhong, 33–34
Zhou Enlai, 46
Zhu Hailun, 128
Zoroastrianism, 8

Zunghar Mongols 1, 12–13; disappearance of, 14
Zungharia (Yili), 3, 10, 18
Zuo Zongtang, 17–18

CPSIA information can be obtained
at www.ICGtesting.com
Printed in the USA
BVHW071709291021
620254BV00002B/10

9 781538 162989